VALUATIONS

A Line by Line Look at the Intricacies of Term Sheets & Valuations

By,
Alex Wilmerding

THOMSON REUTERS®

For Customer Assistance Call 1-800-328-4880

Mat #42111678

ISBN 978-1-539-22982-7

About the Author

Alex Wilmerding is a Principal at Pantheon Ventures, where he evaluates investment opportunities and monitors investments in Asia, focusing on infrastructure, venture, growth and buyouts. He has served on the Pantheon Global Co-investment Committee, as a member of the Asia Investment Committee and on Advisory Boards and Committees of private equity funds across Asia. Alex also manages business development and client services in the Asian region for Pantheon. He is based in Hong Kong. Prior to joining Pantheon, Alex was a Director at Citi Private Bank with a focus working with financial sponsors including private equity and venture funds. He previously spent nine years as a partner at Boston Capital Ventures where he sourced, structured and managed investments in the areas of business process outsourcing and distribution, as well as the areas of information technology, hospitality and transportation services. At Boston Capital Ventures, he served as a director on the boards of portfolio companies including HUBX, Inc., a Waltham, Massachusetts based revenue management and distribution services solutions provider to the hospitality industry, which was sold to Sabre, after merging with SynXis Corporation; KhiMetrics, Inc., a Scottsdale, AZ based developer of revenue management solutions sold to SAP; FareChase, Inc., a web-based travel solutions company sold to Yahoo!; and Wandrian, Inc., a rail inventory distribution services company. Wilmerding also served as an observer to the boards of Exa Corporation, EXA (NASDAQ), the now public, Bedford, MA based developer of fluid flow simulation software for wind tunnel applications, and Vectrix Corporation, the New Bedford, MA based advanced transportation solutions provider. In the not-for-profit arena, Wilmerding has served as an Officer and Trustee of the Yale-China Association, an organization based in New Haven, CT which facilitates educational, environmental, legal and medical exchanges between the United States and China. Prior to Boston working for Boston Capital Ventures, he served as Commercial Manager Eastern China for the Fednav Group, as well as in executive management positions for Cathay Pacific Airways and Dragonair in Hong Kong, Shanghai and Jakarta. Wilmerding earned his B.A. in history from Yale University and his M.B.A. in Finance and Organizational Management from the Columbia Business School. Questions or comments regarding this book can be addressed to wilmerding@hotmail.com.

Table of Contents

Chapter 1

Term Sheet Basics

§ 1:1 What is a term sheet?

In the venture capital community, a term sheet outlines the terms for a deal; it serves as a letter of intent given to a company seeking investment by a private equity or "venture" firm in order to outline the proposed terms for an investment transaction between the two parties. A term sheet has two important functions: it summarizes the important financial and legal terms related to a contemplated transaction; and it quantifies, both in numbers and qualified terms, the value of the transaction or the venture capital financing. If the terms for a financing as captured in the term sheet are agreed to by the entrepreneur and the investor who presents it, the document then serves as the basis on which to draft the legal documents surrounding the class of the securities contemplated by the financing and to make modifications to the articles of incorporation of the company where necessary.

Typically, term sheets are used by venture capital investors as well as institutional investors or syndicates of angel investors in their discussions and negotiations with prospective investees. Outside of the venture capital context, term sheets can be used for any business development or financing deal. For example, a company contemplating a contract with a potential business partner can capture the terms of a proposed relationship in a term sheet. The value of a term sheet is its ability to focus parties in a deal on the essence of the deal prior to initiating costly legal drafting and to move them to close the transaction. Term sheets are most often produced by the venture firm that is making its initial investment in a private company. The firm or individual investor who puts out the term sheet is usually the lead investor in a venture investment round. Take, for example, a company that has been founded by management and has only common stock. The founder or core of executive management of that company will approach prospective angel and venture investors in the hope that those investors will be interested enough in making an investment that they will draft a term sheet and present that to the company.

Once drafted, the term sheet becomes an expression of a group of investors' interest in investing in a company as well as an outline of the terms by which they are interested in investing. It is typically presented to that prospective investee's CEO. As part of the process of agreeing on the terms of a term sheet, the two parties (the investors and the CEO or core executive team of the firm seeking funding) participate in a series of discussions, with the expectation from the investors that the company will accept their proposed terms. Term sheets are almost always negotiated. Even in situations in which companies are hotly sought after by venture investors, term sheets will likely be subject to negotiation.

A term sheet is not a complete description of a deal. However comprehensive parties may intend or interpret the language drafted to be, some number of points in a final contract could change the essence or meaning of points captured in the term sheet. It is therefore important to completely review and assess final documentation.

§ 1:2 Magnified importance

In the venture capital community, the importance of a term

sheet is magnified when a round requires an amount of capital greater than that which one investor alone is willing to provide. In these instances, the term sheet allows an entrepreneur, CEO, or management team to gain a commitment from one investor and use that investor as a reference point to bring aboard other investors as part of a syndicate that commits to invest the required amount of capital. This is particularly important in the later stages of a company's life in those instances when a term sheet is initiated by investors who had participated in prior rounds of a company's financing. For example, in weak markets, companies may be unsuccessful in attracting new capital and a new investor at a time when additional capital is required by the company. In order to do so, it may be necessary for an existing investor or group of investors to come up with a term sheet and float it to the company.

Typically, investors from prior rounds of financings are prepared to invest in subsequent rounds because they both believe in the company's prospects and want to ensure that a new round of financing does not dilute their original interest in the company. Unless of course a company is fabulously successful, the amount that an investor or group of investors will commit to investing in rounds subsequent to their initial round of investment will typically be only a portion of the contemplated subsequent round. In the event that a company is struggling to raise that round, existing investors who float a term sheet will do so under terms that are attractive when compared to prior rounds, called a down round, or represent a round at the same price as the prior round, called a flat round.

§ 1:3 Written in stone?

A term sheet is not technically a binding legal document particularly if the text states explicitly that it is not legally binding. However, as a matter of contract law, both parties have an implied duty to negotiate in good faith. For legal and reputational reasons, it is important that a term sheet states very clearly which parts are binding and which parts are not. Where language includes words like "agree", language can be held to be legally enforceable and once signed by both parties reflect an implicit agreement between the two parties to proceed to a financing subject to the terms incorporated in the term sheet. A breach of terms subsequent to a negotiation may not only give rise to reputational damage but could potentially cloud a future negotiation. The more reputable the venture firm and the more ethical the entrepreneur the more likely the essence of the term sheet will be preserved and remain binding up until the closing of a financing.

Term sheets often include an exclusivity clause. This requires the company, once it has accepted the term sheet, not to solicit competing term sheets from other venture firms or syndicates. For as long as language in the term sheet clearly states it is non-binding and language drafted is careful not to imply any agreement, an entrepreneur can in effect retain an "out". There is little legal recourse for a prospective investor if the language makes clear that the term sheet does not reflect any actual or implicit agreement.

The tenor and nature of the relationship that is established between prospective investors and a company is critical to the strength of the term sheet and the extent to which it remains binding through to a financing. From a reputable venture firms perspective, the assumption is that once a term sheet has been agreed upon and due diligence commences, the deal is going to be consummated on an agreed timetable (in many cases it can take two to four weeks of legal drafting for a round to be finalized). In the rare situation in which investors or the company moves to revisit and diverge from the terms after the term sheet has been agreed upon, the bedrock of the relationship between investors and a company is challenged, sometimes irreparably.

§ 1:4 The only thing constant is change

Even so, a term sheet is not a living, breathing document that lasts beyond a financing. A term sheet accepted by the entrepreneur and the investor who is proposing it works as a summary or outline that is used to draft the legal documents surrounding the new class of securities that are contemplated in a round of financing and to make modifications to the articles of incorporation of the company, also known as the company's charter. While common stock may be owned by the founders and angel investors, venture investors will typically call for a new class of stock, called preferred stock, to be issued when they invest. A new class of stock can be issued during each round of investment; the terms will vary depending upon the strength and state of the company. The terms of each round of financing may affect previous classes of stock and the legal language that dictates the powers related to those previous classes of shares. As a result, powers that were granted to existing shareholders may need to be changed or modified as a result of the terms proposed by a new round of investors before a round of financing can be consummated.

For example, a new investor may want to receive a class of securities that have a liquidation preference, the right to be paid back before other investors. The corporate charter will dictate whether investors holding previous classes of securities have to agree to allow a new class of shares to have terms or powers superior to theirs. The new investor may propose that he wants those powers only for his class of securities, but the entrepreneurs and previous investors may say that the a new class of shares can't have them unless prior classes are allowed them as well. So, it is critical that the term sheet reflect a clear understanding of a company's capital structure and the expectations and understanding of the business by existing shareholders.

After the term sheet is agreed to, the lawyers have to redraft and make amendments to the company's articles of incorporation in order to reflect any changes required by the new class of shares created by a round of financing and to make any changes to the powers of existing classes of shares. To the extent that they are empowered to, investors holding prior classes of stock whose powers are amended as a result of a new financing will need to agree with proposed changes. During the drafting process, the term sheet gives the lawyers the framework to draft a Purchase and Sale Agreement, the document that the investors in the new round will sign, and to make amendments to the company's charter or articles of incorporation. Any amendment to the articles of incorporation that compromises the powers of existing classes of shareholders requires a vote by all the shareholders and directors before the amendment to the article of incorporation can be made and the financing proceeds.

Once the documents surrounding a financing, typically the Purchase and Sales Agreement and revised Certificate of Incorporation, have been prepared and signed off, the company gets back to its usual course of business and the term sheet is no longer relevant to the life of the company. It is just a part of the history of the company's financing.

§ 1:5 Finding a term sheet that fits

As is the case in any investment, terms and conditions will vary widely. So much, in fact, that one could compare an initial template (see Chapter Three) with a final term sheet and see few similarities. The reason that term sheets vary so much is that the context in which each company finds itself is different. The competitive profile of every company is different; its management team and list of customers, for example, will have different values or merits depending upon the bias of each group of investors. The investment climate at the time of each contemplated financing will also vary.

So context is really what dictates the contents of a term sheet. It is the context in which an investment finds itself or is placed that will determine the profile of a term sheet and the extent to which terms appear fair or more favorable to the investors or to the company.

Term sheets have evolved from following five basic forms and styles 20 years ago to following all shapes and sizes. Term sheets have evolved to vary in format and style. The fact that a prospective investor does not use a specific firm is not necessarily a red flag to a venture or private equity firm; countless law firms firms have developed reputable venture practices and have adopted term sheet styles that follow similar formats. Nevertheless, selecting a law firm inexperienced in venture capital or private equity financings could seriously handicap an entrepreneur in the process of negotiation. It is as important to confirm the experience of the firm one contemplates selecting as the partner at the firm one will work with.

Because a term sheet is basically an outline for a transaction and reflects the style of the legal firm used by the investor, there can be anywhere from eight to 15 sections. There are many variables within each of these sections in terms of legal language, which can be changed and substituted so that there is an exponential number of term sheets that one could devise. So the structure of term sheets will be similar in nature, but the language and effective result can vary significantly.

§ 1:6 Investors: institutional versus angel term sheets

Term sheets written by institutional investors, which includes venture capital firms and large corporations, are likely to vary from those offered by angel investors, who often do not offer term sheets at all. Angel investors typically invest during the very early stages of a company, use their own private capital, and may invest in chunks of $10,000 to $250,0000. Angels are typically buying common stock, the same class of stock owned by founders. That sort of individual may be fluent in the terms and conditions that venture and corporate investors use but is not likely to dwell on legal parlance in a term sheet to the extent that later stage venture investors will. Angels are classed as such because they are willing to assume greater risk at a time when the future of a company's business is more uncertain. It is therefore less likely that they will be able to secure from entrepreneurs terms that require a company to meet very specific and exact hurdles in terms of financial performance.

Angel networks and angel investors themselves have however become more sophisticated. It is entirely plausible that one angel or several could work together to provide an entrepreneur a pool of capital and in so doing require that their capital be treated differently from that of the entrepreneur who would hold common stock. In this instance, the angel investor or investors would probably provide a term sheet but given the early stage of the company, the framework of the term sheet would likely be quite simple.

The process of working with angel investors who purchase common stock on an individual basis is likely to be more informal, because angels who are experienced will typically assume that the rights of common stockholders will be a subject for negotiation when the company entertains a later round of venture investing. Having said this, it serves the company well to incorporate in its charters a host of rights to common stockholders; while they can always be negotiated out at a later stage, it is easier to establish them for common stock holders at the outset than to try to negotiate to incorporate them at a later stage.

Angel money, if sophisticated, will typically assume that there will be subsequent rounds of financing and enormous potential for change in the profile of a company; it is therefore less practical for angels who typically invest in smaller amounts and not as syndicates to negotiate preferential terms and to slow the work of a company down by requiring companies to issue new classes of preferred stock at a stage when growth and time to market are critical. At the time of an investment by a venture investor, however, term sheets take on an important role for the venture investor who is looking to capture expectations in terms of the company's revenue performance and profitability and the way in which liquidation or exit will be handled by the company.

§ 1:7 Corporate responsibility

The objective for financial return for an institutional investor (corporate or venture) is similar to that of the angel investor, but an institutional investor's primary concern is its own fiduciary responsibility to its outside investors. A key issue for an institutional investor is how the terms of its participation, dictated in the term sheet, will enable the investment firm to work within the guidelines of its own investment mandate. This is why a time frame spelled out clearly on a term sheet is so important to an institutional investor.

Entrepreneurs seeking funding must understand that venture and corporate investors have limited partners or shareholders to speak to. In the case of the venture investor, which primarily work as limited partnerships, their partners dictate that they will only operate as a partnership for a restricted number of years. In some cases it is as limited as five years with a two year extension; in other cases its as long as 10 years with the ability to extend for one or two years. These limited partners, whether they be pension funds or wealthy individuals, will expect to contribute their capital over a relatively short number of years (one to four), and they will expect to see returns within three to seven years.

As venture capitalists (VCs) propose a term sheet to a company they are naturally going to try to include terms that will encourage the way the company operates to reflect the time frame to liquidity that the venture investor is looking to receive. In other words, the company is expected to meet its financial responsibility to the venture firm in the investor's necessary time frame. This can be managed or expressed in certain clauses within a term sheet. The most obvious one is called a milestone section, in which a venture investor will set strict milestones in terms of when a company should have performed or achieved certain levels of revenues or numbers of contracts that are assumed to be each yielding certain revenue, and at what time. This stages the infusion of capital. For example, an investor can milestone a $10 million syndication of capital so that the capital is contributed to the company in two or three lump sums based on the company achieving certain levels of revenue and sales.

§ 1:8 In the driver's seat

When entrepreneurs receive their first term sheet, they should consult their lawyer and decide whether the economics of the deal are close to what they expected them to be. If so, they should ask the lawyer or the lawyer of the venture investor to draft the necessary securities documents related to the new class of shares.

If the economics of the deal is not up to the entrepreneurs' expectations, the term sheet enables the entrepreneurs to potentially seek other investors; in other words, accelerate the process of getting the right financing. But entrepreneurs may go about this the wrong way. Assuming there is no exclusivity clause in the term sheet, which is intended to prevent them from continuing to shop a deal, some may meet with a prospective investor and say, "We have a commitment at a pre-money valuation of X, but we really want Y; we don't think they will give us that amount. Your firm is a better fit for us; it has strengths the other firm doesn't." This is not the best approach. The venture capital community is small and tight-knit. Many deals are done together, so turning your back on one firm means potentially turning your back on everybody. Even if an entrepreneur considers a term sheet non-binding, whether or not it has an exclusivity clause, shopping the deal has the risk of undermining his credibility and reputation with the firm that has already submitted a term sheet to him. It's better to look for a firm that brings a host of positives and meet at some reasonable middle ground on valuation, because the nature of the relationship that evolves during a term sheet negotiation will be carried forward throughout the life of a company should an investor agree to consummate a deal, and should a term sheet result in financing.

On the other hand, it's possible to shop for financing the way one might shop for a car: You are trying to find the dealer with the best price, and they all have Audi's. That's normal. In a financing, the entrepreneur may approach two firms simultaneously and work with the one that commits to the dollar amount that solves all his financial goals.

The smartest entrepreneur is working several venture firms simultaneously, looking either to have one of them finance the deal in entirety or to bring them together to finance the deal as a group. This is likely to happen when an entrepreneur is looking for financing and either can't find a firm that will provide the entire amount or doesn't want a firm to provide the entire amount. The entrepreneur may receive a term sheet from an investor willing to give 25 percent of the round, then he can use that term sheet to help attract investors willing to partner with the lead investment firm and cover the remaining 75 percent.

Chapter 2

How to Examine a Term Sheet

§ 2:1 Under the looking glass

It is critical to consult experienced counsel prior to agreeing to a term sheet. But while a lawyer is examining the economics of the deal spelled out in the term sheet, the entrepreneur should be conducting his own examination of the terms. If the term sheet is balanced and fairly aligns the interests of investors and the company, it will typically not have substantive effects on the company—if the company performs to or exceeds expectations and meets milestones that have been agreed upon or represented in the company's business plan. Nevertheless, there are a few terms and sections to which the entrepreneur should give extra attention. For the purposes of discussion, the section names to which I will refer correspond to the term sheet framework and style provided by the Boston offices of Kirkpatrick and Lockhart.

The most obvious section that requires extra attention is the price per share. Price per share is important because it embodies the economic value of where the company is today. It is possible to do a simple equation to determine what the price per share converts to in terms of pre-money or post-money valuation for the company.

The Current Securities Section (which describes all shares and the number of shares in each class of stock that have existed before the round that is being contemplated) gives the investor's summary of the company's capital structure and will typically include not only existing shares but a summary of any warrants and options issued. The calculation of pre-money value should be the result of multiplying the total number of shares outstanding, including warrants and issued options, by the price per share that is offered in the term sheet. The post-money valuation, on an as-converted basis, is determined by adding the total amount to be raised in equity in the round of financing contemplated by the term sheet to the pre-money valuation. The post-money value placed on a company at the time of the term sheet discussions embeds some expectations for performance of the company over time. So one can look quickly to the value placed on the company, examine the company's expectations as to how it's going to perform in terms of revenue numbers and profitability over subsequent one to three years, and consider what values the company may command at future periods of time either in a sale or in a future financing. Then one can calculate what that means in terms of a multiple or rate of return over a period of years on the investment. If a venture investor is looking to achieve a gross return of 50 percent and a net return after fees in the 35 percent range, the relationship between the post-money valuation and the value of the company at time of exit are critical in the VC's calculation of expected return.

§ 2:2 Corporate governance

It's also vital to inspect the terms in the Board Composition and Meetings as well as Special Board Approval Items sections that concern corporate governance and the way in which the company's executive team and board of directors will be expected to interact. These terms help investors, who are close enough to the company and have done enough due diligence, immediately see the way in which certain types of actions and powers, if held by certain members of the board, could be useful in affecting how the company is managed in certain critical circumstances.

When examining these sections, it is important to review who the directors are and which classes of stock will be represented by which seats or individuals. It is also necessary to consider how many executives, members of management teams, and founders are represented on the board, and the total number of board members. This information is critical, because as classes of shares are issued subsequent to each financing, each class will typically require one or several board seats and the right to influence certain actions of the company. Additionally, a board that has a majority influence by founders and individuals who are related to founders may be less attractive to a sophisticated institutional investor at any stage of investment unless the majority of individuals on the board alongside the VC are clearly established industry names with a depth of experience and are respected independent thinkers. The degree of influence that a board can have over the direction of a company is diluted unless a board has a balance of management, independent industry experts, and financial investors.

In later-stage investments, the board composition and meetings section gets more complex, because a company that initially offered only common stock and possibly one class of preferred stock may experience one or more subsequent rounds of preferred financings. This will affect the board composition, because as more investors become involved, their expectations will need to be represented. The degree to which management is executing comes under increasingly greater scrutiny by the investors.

For all of these reasons, it is necessary to inspect the Special Board Approval Items section for any powers that existing board members hold. Often board members representing preferred stock or a majority of the shareholders of a class of preferred stock (the shares that venture investors typically purchase) will expect to have approval rights in the event that the company contemplates such actions as taking on debt above certain modest levels, say $250,000; making significant management hires; or engaging in a merger or acquisition. Entrepreneurs are naturally loathe to give up the freedom to make certain operating decisions, however VCs expect their level of influence to be high, particularly over areas that could significantly affect the company's capital structure or profitability.

§ 2:3 Don't get held up

Another sticking point in a term sheet is options and the way in which they are treated and valued in a pre- or post-money valuation. There can be extreme differences in opinion as to how many options should be issued in order to accommodate future growth.

A company can have great plans for doubling the size of its workforce within a 12-month period. But after financing, say it has 10,000 shares outstanding, only 5 percent of which are options, all of which are granted, the company may need to create another 15 percent of options for new employees. Or, founding management who has founder shares may ask to be treated as employees. Those who do so are effectively double dipping. They want to keep their founder shares but also want to be awarded as employees, so they ask for a percentage in terms of options. Suddenly the contemplated valuation of the company can change by 10 to 20 percent, depending on the future expectations for the company.

Essentially, founders see themselves getting diluted during each subsequent financing. Although dilution is a typical part of each subsequent round of financing, they sometimes want to be awarded options for their roles as employees. If they do, the founders should be prepared to raise the bar and tie additional options awards to improved performance and greater shareholder value.

§ 2:4 Red flags

Price per share, corporate governance, options, and valuation are all key areas of a term sheet that entrepreneurs need to inspect thoroughly. But they are not the only areas to watch. Entrepreneurs must look out for the many possible red flags any term sheet may have. The three biggest are as follows:

1) **Underfinancing** One red flag is if an amount of money offered by an investor is lower than the dollar amount the entrepreneur feels he or she reasonably needs to get through the next phase of growth and to a subsequent financing at a reasonable subsequent valuation.

This strategy may benefit the company seeking financing, but it has drawbacks and attendant risks unless it is a carefully crafted part of a long-term financing strategy. It may also benefit the VC. The VC can ensure that the value of the company will rise if, by requiring an entrepreneur to accept a lower dollar amount in a round, the entrepreneur is then able to bring in a strategic investor later on to secure additional financing for the company and do so at a higher valuation. The downside comes about if the strategy doesn't work out and the company fails to attract capital in a later round for any number of reasons. Should the market change, investors might, in a competitive financing market, conclude that one of the reasons a prior round was small was because the company's business model had not been compelling enough to attract sufficient numbers of investors. Similarly, a sector can lose its luster or suffer a general re-evaluation by the VC and corporate strategic investment community. Under such circumstances when a company cannot attract new investors on better terms, its existing round of investors may seek to protect themselves by investing money on preferential terms.

Encouraging companies to pursue business plans which assume subsequent rounds of financing within relatively short periods of time can be an effective way for VCs to motivate companies and to ensure that their funding is provided at intervals rather than up front. But it is wiser for entrepreneurs to seek funding which will last them 12 to 18 months in competitive financing environments. This does not mean that financing for this period of time need necessarily be secured in one payment up front. A syndicate of investors with the capability of investing funds in several tranches can enable the entrepreneur a 12- to 18-month period of funding; the challenge for the entrepreneur is to assemble a syndicate with this capability, but under an initial valuation that leaves room for future funding.

2) Limitations to the Scope of a Syndicate Another red flag is investors who try to dissuade an entrepreneur from opening a round or increasing it in size in order to accommodate other interested VCs. Some investors may do so only to maximize influence and control by that VC firm or to take as much of a good thing as they can get. There may, however, be legitimate reasons for a VC to do so: Not all VCs work well together; certain round sizes may also become too small to justify the overhead that may be required to administer an investment.

The other practical downside in not opening a syndicate that includes several venture firms is that a company may limit its options when it looks for follow-on rounds of financing. Presumably, the more diverse the profile of a syndicate the higher the likelihood of more introductions to other VC firms in a future round of financing.

One simple rule in any financing for entrepreneurs is this: It is often wise to take funding from interested investors when you are offered it. The fundraising process is distracting and eats up precious time and resources.

3) Milestones Milestones can be a reasonable approach to constructing a term sheet; they can also be a serious red flag. For some entrepreneurs, any milestone set by an investor in a term sheet is a red flag. Investors typically milestone a deal by writing into a term sheet the commitment to fund, but only in allotments and based upon specific financial performance prior to subsequent rounds of funding. Investors might provide $10 million in commitments in four quarterly payments, for example, enabling the investors to revisit the performance of the company at the time of each quarter's funding payment. From the view of an entrepreneur, everybody participating in an early stage company typically should accept that it is a highly risky venture. Opportunities as perceived today can change quickly, and companies may need to retrench and revisit assumptions.

What's more, management is taking additional risks by committing to a highly risky venture. Not surprisingly, management will want to have the flexibility to be able to change course as necessary, rather than to find out that in two or three months, should the company not be meeting their plan for unanticipated and understandable reasons, an institutional or venture investor who has prescribed this power can basically take over control of the company, boot management and bring in new management, or curtail the investment entirely.

Even so, goals that require a company to meet at a minimum 50 percent or 75 percent of plan should be achievable—particularly in expansion and later stage deals—barring enormous cyclical shifts in the economy or in a sector. At the end of the day, if a company can't meet a majority of its plan, particularly when due to factors within the company's control, the company is not performing.

Clearly, a key reason investors like to use milestones is that by setting milestones they can put in place a framework which can provide downside protection for them. In the event the firm doesn't reach certain targets there can be a conversion ratio that will allow the preferred investors to have an adjustment in the percentage of the company they own. With a downside protection clause investors will set a date by which certain targets are expected to have been met. For example, if actual revenues for a period are below 75 percent of a target, a conversion ratio could kick in to adjust the number of shares that they own in the round recently issued so that the value of their ownership as struck in a recent round of financing is adjusted to reflect actual performance. A second hurdle could require the share price to be adjusted further under a more demanding formula in the event the company fails to reach revenue targets of 50 percent of plan. An entrepreneur can be comfortable with these conversion ratios if a company's plan is eminently achievable, and there is little perceived risk associated with doing so. However, the entrepreneur has to be careful to ensure that the manner and way in which the company's financial performance will be recognized is stipulated. Something as simple as a change in the way Generally Accepted Accounting Principles (GAAP) recognizes revenues could trigger an adjustment to share pricing, unless language stipulating the contrary has been incorporated into documentation. It's vital to ensure that the term sheet articulates the standards, or references standards given elsewhere, and shows an example. If standards change and an investor wants to take advantage of such a clause, the entrepreneur may be setting himself up for a legal challenge.

Although milestones are a red flag, they are also negotiable. But depending upon a company's circumstances and the funding environment, other issues may be more important negotiation points for the entrepreneur.

§ 2:5 Red flags for investors

As much as milestones are a source of discomfort for entrepreneurs, red flags for prospective investors could include strong resistance by a company to be subject to of milestones and a potential adjustment to investor ownership in the event a company does not meet milestones or refusal to accept funding in tranches. If the stage of the investment is so early that a revenue plan is clearly unpredictable, it might be unreasonable for an investor to expect an entrepreneur to accept tight milestones. But if a company is a relatively later or expansion stage opportunity with a high degree of predictable revenues and a sufficiently rich pre-money valuation, it is understandable that an investor may consider an entrepreneur's intransigence on this issue disconcerting at best or a no-go at worst.

The category of Special Board Approval Items that are defined by venture investors in term sheets is another area about which VCs will be somewhat stubborn. Fiduciary responsibility to ensuring a modicum of influence over the course of an investment, particularly when an investment is not going to plan, makes these issues particularly important to an investor and a source of significant concern when an entrepreneur looks to remove them from a proposed term sheet.

Board composition is likewise as significant an issue for investors as it is for entrepreneurs. When a venture investor is in the business of trying to predict to some high degree of probability a successful financial outcome, he wants to know that the future course of the company is relatively clear and that as many tools as possible are provided to him to influence that future when necessary. If a board is composed of a majority of advisors and friends of the firm who do not have close alignment with the interests of shareholders in maximizing value, the VC is going to want to see a change that creates some sort of balance that more closely aligns the board with the goals of a majority of shareholders. To a VC, a board requires a balance of management, independent industry experts, and financial investors.

A variety of other areas can also cause VCs to seriously reconsider an investment. Protection in the event of liquidation, found in the Liquidation Preference section of a term sheet, is a critical area for investors. Entrepreneurs need to remember that if pricing is fair or aggressive, downside risk will be one area which VCs will focus on.

Limitations in the Information Rights section will also be a red flag for investors. Entrepreneurs rightfully do not want to spend a majority of their time reporting to VCs. Nevertheless, entrepreneurs who are too controlling and resist providing an investor with the right to a full audit of the company's operations or even a reasonable level of access by VCs to company information risk turning off investors completely. The way this section is handled and negotiated could signal to the investor that the entrepreneur may want to try to hide something in the future or may be difficult to work with.

To avoid creating a red flag for investors, entrepreneurs must look for balance and flexibility when negotiating terms.

§ 2:6 Beware of strategic partners that become investors

A final red flag, for both investors and entrepreneurs, is when a firm's strategic partner is interested in becoming an investor in that company. A strategic partner that is also an investor can put a company in a compromising position for two primary reasons. First, the strategic partner can require up front certain rights or powers to influence or block future partnerships or a sale or acquisition of a company, whether or not its investment is staged. These red flags would typically show up in the Special Board Approval Items section. The amount and nature of an equity investment from a strategic partner can put off future potential partners and acquirers. The term sheet is the entrepreneur's first opportunity to see what the true intentions of a strategic partner may be.

Second, if the partner's investment is staged and the company's business model is too dependent upon the strategic partner, the company can unknowingly limit its choices and independence down the road. Certainly, a strategic partner can offer a host of distribution channels as well as product collaboration opportunities. But it is critical that a company's business plan is not so dependent on a strategic partner that a staged investment by that partner could allow the partner to renegotiate terms unfairly when a later stage of the investment comes due. So the core goals of one's business plan need to be considered carefully when analyzing the terms and conditions incorporated into a term sheet by a strategic investor.

Chapter 3

A Section-by-Section View of a Term Sheet

§ 3:1 What is a term sheet?

In the venture capital community, a term sheet is basically a letter of intent prepared by a venture capital firm to summarize all the important financial and legal terms related to a transaction and to quantify the value of the transaction or the venture capital financing. A term sheet serves as an outline of a transaction. The most important commercial and legal terms are typically captured ineight to 15 sections. (There are 16 sections in the sample term sheet presented in Figures 1 to 18 in this chapter.) There are many variables within each section, in terms of legal language, so that there is an exponential number of term sheets that one could draw up. Many of these sections can be written either to favor the investor, to favor the entrepreneur, or in a balanced manner so as to benefit both parties as fairly as possible.

Every entrepreneur contemplating venture financing needs to understand the degrees to which sections of a term sheet are either Company or Investor Favorable. This section has been designed to provide a range of examples of how many sections of a term sheet can be either Company Favorable, Investor Favorable, or Middle of the Road. Where appropriate, examples are labeled Investor Favorable, Middle of the Road, and Company Favorable. A term sheet would only have one clause, not all three, but the format used here is intended to provide entrepreneurs with a clear picture as to how any one of the three types of clauses can vary the economic and qualitative effect of the investor's offering.

§ 3:2 The preamble

In a preamble to a term sheet there can be certain exclusions or assumptions as to the length of time that a term sheet will remain in place, and provisions as to the entrepreneur's ability to shop a deal to other investors.

There may be a paragraph that states that during a period commencing on a given date, the company's directors, employees, and representatives may not contact, solicit, engage in any discussions, enter in any agreement, or furnish any information to anyone other than the investors or representative of investors, without prior written consent. This type of language effects a quiet period or lock-up period during which the term sheet should not be discussed with third parties or other term sheets solicited. This type of language must be crystal clear about what parts are enforceable and which parts are not. If the language isn't clear, some elements might be interpreted to be enforceable.

§ 3:3 Opening information

The first paragraph of a term sheet is fairly standard (see Figure 1). In fact, quite often that first paragraph doesn't even exist. Instead the term sheet might simply have a title that gives the name of the company being funded, a subtitle that reads "A Summary of Terms for Proposed Private Placement of (name of stock—Series A Preferred Stock, for example), and the name of the stock issuer, which would be the name of the company that would be receiving the investment from the venture capitalist or syndicate of investors. But the first paragraph is a good way of summarizing what is in the document and of providing an overview of the nature of the transaction contemplated. If the term sheet is going to be read by people who aren't close to the transaction, the opening paragraph clarifies the nature of the situation.

In the example below, [____] Ventures, L.P. would refer to the typical name of a venture capital firm's fund, each of which typically are limited partnerships, here abbreviated as L.P. The bracket referring to the "Investors" could include the name of individuals or corporate investors who may be investing as a syndicate alongside the venture fund.

FIGURE 1

[Company Name]
[Term Sheet Date]

MEMORANDUM OF TERMS FOR PRIVATE PLACEMENT OF EQUITY SECURITIES

General

[________] Ventures, L.P., and [ ] (the "Investors") are prepared to invest $ [________________________] million in [ ] (the "Company") under the terms contained in this term sheet. With the exception of the section of this agreement relating to expenses, this term sheet is a non-binding document prepared for discussion purposes only, and the proposed investment is specifically subject to customary stock purchase agreements, legal due diligence, and other conditions precedent contained herein, all satisfactory to the Investors in their sole discretion.

[Other Company or deal specific terms.]

---

§ 3:4 New securities offered

The New Securities Offered section, which appears at the top of Figure 2, at first appears to be self-explanatory. It is critical, however, that an entrepreneur understand the differences between different classes of securities and what the implications are of the type of security contemplated by a proposed offering. Figure 2 assumes that Series A Preferred will be offered.

In order of priority, common stock usually holds no special powers, it's just ordinary stock with one vote exercisable per share in the event a shareholder vote is called. Preferred stock takes a more senior position in the company's capital structure, which means it usually has some rights attached to it that give it preference, for dividend or liquidation treatment, over common stock and usually has corporate governance powers that common stock does not hold. There can be multiple series of preferred stock. As each subsequent financing transpires, it is often appropriate to issue a new series of preferred stock at the time of each transaction in order to provide that series with the rights and pricing that is appropriate at that point in the life of the company. Assuming the life and value of a company is not static, Purchase Price Per Share for each new class of stock will typically differ at each subsequent offering, substantiating the need to issue new classes of securities at each successive financing. The Preferred Shares are usually convertible to common.

Typically, for example, common stock is issued when a company is founded. Everybody shares in the same level of risk. It's just common stock, meaning angel investors and founders receive common shares on equal terms. A company grows in size and sophistication and then tries to attract new money. A successive round of funding might involve a venture or corporate investor. Preferred shares will be issued to those investors, because the pricing and value of the shares will presumably be different from that of the common shares. At the very least, the investors in a successive round will require certain levels of influence and rights that the common shareholders do not hold.

Those investors, having agreed to finance the company on different terms from the common, ask for certain rights, in terms of influence. This is done to compensate for what is typically a minority position at a higher price than common or to retain a level of influence over whether the company entertains future financings, on what terms those financings may occur, and in the event that the company doesn't perform or meet the expectations, over how and when the company may need to be liquidated. Allocating a certain number of seats on the board that are attributable to that series of preferred investors is one way of securing influence. So if there were five board members before the preferred shares are issued for example, the company might agree to ask two existing board members to step down in order to issue two new board seats to the investors of that preferred round. The board could also be expanded.

Unless there is a change in the future board composition that is agreed to by the preferred investors, they will always keep those seats and always have that level of influence. In fact, they will probably ask that the company's charter is changed to reflect an agreed upon number of seats. In this way, if any change in size of the board or an event which could contemplete preferred stock converted to common, the preferred investors would have to agree; if they did not, the company's charter typically could not be amended.

Assuming that the company's articles of incorporation reflect that there will be a five-person board, the preferred investors are being assured of retaining a 40 percent influence at the board level. In this example, the investors as a class of preferred stock could therefore only have a 15 percent interest in the company and yet retain close to a majority of control at the board level. In fact, if one of the remaining three board members is an independent, it would be possible that the "block" could retain a controlling influence on the board.

In some cases new classes of stocks will have the same rights as all previous preferred series of shares. So a B could be issued after an A, and the B investors have the same rights as the A. In this case, the pricing and board representation might be the only difference. But typically, the lower in the alphabet the series of shares, the more influence the most recent series might have over that company and the higher the likelihood that all existing preferred shares are sharing any rights they have with that current round. So either the most current round has more influence, or at the very least, shares all the rights of a previous round.

The most significant change will be in valuation. The higher in the alphabet series of shares, most probably the lower the price of the shares if a company is performing well.

§ 3:5 Total amount raised, number of shares, and purchase price per share

Each of the Total Amount Raised, Number of Shares, and Purchase Price Per Share sections (see Figure 2) is fairly self-explanatory. Total Amount Raised refers to specific elements to the total amount to be raised by the proposed financing; Number of Shares is the number of shares that will result as a result of the proposed financing; and Purchase Price Per Share is the purchase price per share of the shares in the proposed financing. The Total Amount Raised should equal the product of the Number of Shares plus the Purchase Price Per Share.

§ 3:6 Post-financing capitalization

The purpose of the Post-Financing Capitalization section is to summarize what the capital structure of the company will look like after the proposed new financing. Some term sheets include a Current Securities section at the very beginning of the term sheet; in our example (in Figure 1), there is no Current Securities section. Typically, had one been included, no Post-Financing Capitalization would be included in the term sheet; instead the Current Securities section would, when considered together with the New Securities Offered section, provide enough information for the reader to put together a capitalization table. The Post-Financing Capitalization included in Figure 2 summarizes succinctly what the capital structure should look like after the proposed financing and includes summaries of both current and new securities.

The information in this section allows the reader to determine the pre-money and post-money or Total Enterprise Value valuations of the company. To determine the pre-money valuation, one must examine the Post-Financing Capitalization section and multiply the total number of shares—excluding the number of New Securities Offered shares but including the number of options and warrants issued—by the Proposed Purchase Price Per Share noted in Figure 2. To ascertain the post-money valuation or Total Enterprise Value, multiply the number of Total Common Equivalent shares by the Purchase Price Per Share proposed in the term sheet.

It is also possible to determine the Total Common Stock Equivalent number. To do so one should add the number of common stocks, options and warrants, and any preferred stock that had been issued prior to the proposed financing together with the number of shares to be purchased as part of the proposed financing. The Total Common Equivalent assumes that preferred stock and common as well as options and warrants are treated equally in valuing the company. This approach to valuing the company is factually accurate at the time of a financing but may not, when considering preferred stock, reflect the value of preferred stock if converted to common at some point in the future. Preferred stock can, as the next section explains, carry a dividend that could accrue and, in some cases, be added to the original value of the stock should it be paid back under certain circumstances, in liquidation for example.

FIGURE 2

New Securities Offered: Newly issued shares of the Company's Series [A] Preferred (the "Preferred")

Total Amount Raised: [$]

Number of Shares: [/ To be determined to result in the Post-financing Capitalization below.]

Purchase Price Per Share: [$ / To be determined to result in the Post-financing Capitalization below (the "Original Purchase Price").]

Post-Financing Capitalization: Common Stock

Founders:
[Name] [ ]
[Name] [ ]
[Name] [ ]
Sub-Total [ ]

Stock Option Program
[CEO] [ ]
[Others] [ ]
Sub-Total [ ]
Preferred Stock
[________________] Ventures, L.P., [ ]
[Co-Investor(s)] [ ]
Sub-Total [ ]
Total Common Equivalent [ ]

Total Enterprise Value [______]

---

§ 3:7 Dividend provisions

The true value of preferred stock will therefore be a function of a number of provisions detailed throughout the term sheet. Figure 3 highlights the type of clauses that are likely to detail the economic effect that Dividend Provisions can have in increasing the value of preferred stock over time.

Dividend provisions are one of the critical tools that allow VCs to protect their investment and to get out of an investment with at least some prospect of a return in the event of liquidation of the company. The dividend provisions are what the board will live by when they either consider issuing or are required to issue dividends.

There are three dividend provision clauses outlined in Figure 3: Investor Favorable, Middle of the Road, and Company Favorable. Only one form of these three would exist in the term sheet proposed by an investor. These provisions are a mix of weighted variables: neutral, negative, or positive in the favor of investor or company. The differences between the economic effect of the way each of the Investor Favorable, Middle of the Road, and Company Favorable sections are structured is a function of the percentage of return assumed for the preferred stock, whether the dividend is cumulative or non-cumulative, or whether issuance of a dividend for preferred stock should take preference over issuance of a dividend for any existing shares that have rights to dividends.

An entrepreneur must not underestimate the economic effect and difference between cumulative and non-cumulative dividends. If the dividend is non-cumulative and the company doesn't make a decision to issue a dividend in year one, or doesn't have the resources to do so, the subsequent year the slate is clean and the company thereafter is not obligated to make good on the issuance of dividends for any previous years. This means that if the dividend is not issued in year one and a dividend were to be issued in a subsequent year, the company would not be required to issue dividends cumulatively or retroactively for previous years in which the company was unable to issue a dividend.

Let us consider the case of the Investor Favorable example of Dividend Provisions below. As this term sheet details a first round of preferred shares, Series A, the investor would, should the term sheet include the Investor Favorable text in Figure 3, expect to receive dividends at a specific rate of return, in this case at 15 percent. If therefore, dividends were to be issued by the company, dividends would need to be issued to the Series A preferred at a cumulative rate of 15 percent per annum before any dividends could be issued for common shares. Even if the common stock stipulated a return of say 8 percent, this clause would require the board to make a decision to issue dividends to preferred investors. Whatever funds were available would first have to provide the Series A investors with a 15 percent return on their invested capital. Only after this is done would any funds be used to generate a dividend for common stock.

FIGURE 3

Rights, Preferences, and Privileges of the Series [A] Preferred.

(1) Dividend Provisions:
Investor Favorable: The holders of the Series [A] Preferred shall be entitled to receive cumulative dividends in preference to any dividend on the Common Stock at the rate of 15 percent of the Original Purchase Price per annum, when and as declared by the Board of Directors.

Middle of the Road: The holders of the Series [A] Preferred shall be entitled to receive non-cumulative dividends in preference to any dividend on the Common Stock at the rate of 8 percent of the Original Purchase Price per annum, when and as declared by the Board of Directors. The Series [A] Preferred also will participate pro rata in any dividends paid on the Common Stock on an as-converted basis.

Company Favorable: The holders of the Series [A] Preferred shall be entitled to receive non-cumulative dividends in preference to any dividend on the Common Stock at the rate of 8 percent of the Original Purchase Price per annum, when, as and if declared by the Board of Directors.

---

§ 3:8 Liquidation preference

Liquidation means closing down the company. That doesn't necessarily have to be devastating for a VC if appropriate protections have been incorporated into a term sheet. The liquidation preference clause is a tool that enables favorable treatment for preferred shareholders in the event of liquidation.

The most significant variable to consider in the liquidation preference section is the multiple on the value of their initial investment that preferred and common shareholders will receive as a result of this clause (see Figure 4). So, Investor Favorable terms will generally provide the preferred investor a multiple on the value of the initial investment of say three times. In the event of a sale or bankruptcy proceedings, preference would be given to the preferred investor to receive a three-times return on their initial investment, before any proceeds are used to pay anything to any other shareholders, including common shareholders who do not retain these rights. That is in one version of the most investor-favorable situation.

In the case of the Middle of the Road clause in Figure 4, proceeds are distributed so that they are given first to preferred shareholders but in a less preferential manner. The preferred would, in this case, get their original purchase price plus any declared but unpaid dividends. Thereafter, common and preferred shareholders share in proportion to their ownership position the remaining distributions until such time as the preferred has received three times their original purchase price.

VCs are highly sensitive to the time value of money. A return of 3 times over 4 years actually equates to only a 32 percent annualized return. The net return to an investor, when deducting a venture fund's fees, would be below 25 percent, which is not considered an extraordinarily attractive venture capital return.

FIGURE 4

---

(2) Liquidation Preference:

Investor Favorable: In the event of any liquidation or winding up of the Company, the holders of the Series [A] Preferred shall be entitled to receive in preference to the holders of the Common Stock a total liquidation amount equal to [three] times the Original Purchase Price per share plus any declared but unpaid dividends (the "Liquidation Preference"). After the payment of the Liquidation Preference to the holders of the Series [A] Preferred, the remaining assets shall be distributed ratably to the holders of the Common Stock and the Series [A] Preferred on an as converted basis. A merger, acquisition, sale of voting control, or sale of substantially all of the assets of the Company in which the shareholders of the Company do not own a majority of the outstanding shares of the surviving corporation shall be deemed to be a liquidation.

Middle of the Road: In the event of any liquidation or winding up of the Company, the holders of the Series [A] Preferred shall be entitled to receive in preference to the holders of the Common Stock an amount equal to the Original Purchase Price plus any accrued, or declared, but unpaid dividends (the

"Liquidation Preference"). After the payment of the Liquidation Preference to the holders of the Series [A] Preferred, the remaining assets shall be distributed ratably to the holders of the Common Stock and the Series [A] Preferred on a common equivalent basis. A merger, acquisition, or sale of substantially all of the assets of the Company in which the shareholders of the Company do not own a majority of the outstanding shares of the surviving corporation shall be deemed to be a liquidation.

Company Favorable: In the event of any liquidation or winding up of the Company, the holders of the Series [A] Preferred shall be entitled to receive in preference to the holders of the Common Stock an amount equal to the Original Purchase Price (the "Liquidation Preference"). After the payment of the Liquidation Preference to the holders of the Series [A] Preferred, the remaining assets shall be distributed ratably to the holders of the Common Stock. A merger, acquisition, or sale of substantially all of the assets of the Company in which the shareholders of the Company do not own a majority of the outstanding shares of the surviving corporation shall be deemed to be a liquidation.

---

§ 3:9 Redemption

Redemption clauses are the one way for VCs to ensure that a company does not become a lifestyle company that is only in business to give its founders and management a salary or become what VCs consider to be part of the "living dead." Entrepreneurs need to remember that most funds function as limited partnerships with a finite number of years of life. The purpose of the Redemption clause is to provide a structure (see Figure 5) that makes certain that the investors do not invest in companies that are unable to generate liquidity.

The redemption clause puts a finite number of years on the life of an investment, by assuming that the investment is able to generate a return. In so doing it stipulates that at some point in the future if a liquidity event has not happened, then the company will become obligated to redeem the investor's interest in a specific time frame. A liquidity event is a way of providing the investor with a currency through which to phase out of the investment, like a public offering or a buyout that allows the investors' interest to be purchased. Those time frames and variables are stipulated in the examples of Redemption clauses cited in Figure 5. Clauses that are Investor Favorable require redemption relatively rapidly and over a defined and shorter number of years. Clauses that are Middle of the Road are less rapid. The Company Favorable flavor of this clause would of course be no clause at all.

Here is an example of how a redemption clause works: WidgetCompany.com receives $10 million in proceeds from the sale of preferred stock. If on the company's third anniversary it has not generated any opportunity for liquidity for the investor, the Investor Favorable clause requires that, if an election by holders of preferred stock forces them to do so, the company will be required to redeem or pay back one third of the outstanding preferred. In doing so the company must redeem these preferred shares at a rate of three times their Original Purchase Price plus any accrued or unpaid dividends on those shares. In this case the cost to the company would be $10,000,000 after three years plus accrued and unpaid dividends on these shares. The clause goes on to require payment of one half of the outstanding preferred on the fifth anniversary at the same multiple plus accrued and unpaid dividends on this portion of securities. It then requires that remainder of unredeemed shares be treated similarly on the sixth anniversary of the initial investment. The company's management team is basically on notice and reminded that in three years the company must have generated some way in which to pay back investors or it will need to begin to provide them some liquidity so that holders of the stock are not motivated to exercise this right.

This clause in the Investor Favorable format is more stick than carrot. While the three-year wake-up call is more aggressive than what one typically sees in early or expansion stage term sheets, it would make sense for a later stage deal that is expensive and touting to generate liquidity for investors in short order.

The Middle of the Road format is just that. For an early or expansion stage deal it is an eminently reasonable compromise. It is probably generous to rich and more Company Favorable from the VC perspective if the pricing of a deal is expensive and the entrepreneur is pitching liquidity and an exit for the venture investor in less than 5 years time.

FIGURE 5

---

(3) Redemption:

Investor Favorable: Redemption at Option of Investors:

At the election of the holders of at least [a majority] of the Series [A] Preferred, the Company shall redeem 1/3 of the outstanding Series [A] Preferred on the [third] anniversary of the Closing, 1/2 of the outstanding Series [A] Preferred on the fifth anniversary of the Closing and all of the remaining outstanding Series [A] Preferred on the sixth anniversary of the Closing. Such redemptions shall be at a purchase price equal to [three] times the Original Purchase Price plus accrued and unpaid dividends.

Middle of the Road: Redemption at Option of Investors:

At the election of the holders of at least [two thirds] of the Series [A] Preferred, the Company shall redeem the outstanding Series [A] Preferred in three equal annual installments beginning on the [fifth] anniversary of the Closing. Such redemptions shall be at a purchase price equal to the Original Purchase Price plus declared and unpaid dividends.

Company Favorable: None.

---

§ 3:10 Conversion and automatic conversion

Conversion (see Figure 6) is a short clause that is not considered Investor nor Company Favorable, because when conversion happens, it is always assumed to be at an event in which preferred convert to common shares on a 1:1 basis. The purpose of this clause is to enable preferred shareholders to convert in the event of a liquidity event that is likely to generate a return that is higher than the multiple that is prescribed as mandated in the Liquidation Preference section. Investors who are only purchasing preferred stock will often give up their preferred rights if a transaction would yield a higher return. Many of the issues that preferred investors have about control and preferred stock become secondary in a liquidity event that promises them greater upside than that dictated in the Liquidation Preference clauses previously discussed.

Consequently, it is important to consider the relationship between the Liquidation Preference Clause and the Conversion Clause.

In the face of an IPO, the preferred investor will have unique concerns, which are addressed in the Automatic Conversion clause that is proposed in the term sheet. The Automatic Conversion clause, described in Figure 6, specifically describes the range of powers which preferred investors may strive to require in the event a company pushes to go public.

IPOs are not a panacea when it comes to liquidity. A second-rate underwriter who pushes to raise a small amount of money through an IPO could well set a company up to perform poorly on the public markets. If the stock is thinly traded, the preferred investor is left with little ability to trade out of the stock and analysts and market makers have little motivation to follow the stock. Consequently, there are two variables that differentiate the Investor Favorable and Company Favorable clauses in Figure 6. They are the multiple of the original purchase price of the preferred stock at which the preferred will automatically convert into common to facilitate a public offering, and the amount of money that will qualify an IPO as acceptable to the preferred. The preferred investor will contend that the success of the IPO should be measured by the extent to which the multiple on invested cost is high and the amount of money that is raised at IPO.

The choice of language in this clause qualifies the type of underwriter who is likely to be involved in an IPO. The size of the IPO, whether it is Investor Favorable or Company Favorable, scales downwards as it is considered to be more Company Favorable. In the event that a smaller-size offering is contemplated, the type of underwriter is likely to be less established, because the fees involved and the float would only be inviting to a less-established firm.

So the modus operandi of the investor and of management, should an IPO be contemplated that will generate a greater amount of liquidity, is to work together. The higher number of times the original purchase price at which an investor states he will be comfortable converting is really a way for the investor and the investor class to protect itself and to make sure that the IPO will generate liquidity of a certain multiple. It is difficult to generalize, but depending on the investor, investors are looking at a two- to three-year time frame, and a minimum of a three to four times return in that period if not greater. If one considers a net return of 35 percent to the investor in a VC fund to be a goal that an investor may be looking for, the VC will have to return close to 50 percent on all his or his investments in order to produce this return net of fees. An investment would have to do eight times in five years in order to produce a gross return of 52 percent; the effective gross return of the VC's portfolio will of course be significantly lower and the need for the VC to get a return of over 50 percent higher if the success of the one investment must make up for other failed companies in the VC's portfolio. The time value of money weighs heavily in a VC's assessment of an opportunity.

Entrepreneurs' projections of returns are likely to be more aggressive than the actual performance of a company. So when VCs make their predictions and entrepreneurs take exception to what appear to be the aggressive multiples of VCs, what entrepreneurs may fail to accept or realize is that VCs will by their nature be likely to discount an entrepreneurs projections. It is for this reason that milestones can be a middle ground tool in balancing the expectations of VCs and entrepreneurs.

FIGURE 6

---

(4) Conversion: [Investor Favorable, Middle of the Road and Company Favorable are the same.]

The holders of the Series [A] Preferred shall have the right to convert the Series [A] Preferred, at any time, into shares of Common Stock. The initial conversion rate shall be 1:1, subject to adjustment as provided below.

(5) Automatic Conversion:

Investor Favorable: The Series [A] Preferred shall be automatically converted into Common Stock, at the then-applicable conversion price, (i) in the event that the holders of at least two thirds of the outstanding Series [A] Preferred consent to such conversion or (ii) upon the closing of a firmly underwritten public offering of shares of Common Stock of the Company at a per share price not less than [3 times the Original Purchase Price] per share and for a total offering with net proceeds to the Company of not less than $40 million (a "Qualified IPO").

Middle of the Road: The Series [A] Preferred shall be automatically converted into Common Stock, at the then-applicable conversion price, (i) in the event that the holders of at least two thirds of the outstanding Series [A] Preferred consent to such conversion or (ii) upon the closing of a firmly underwritten public offering of shares of Common Stock of the Company at a per share price not less than [2 times the Original Purchase Price] per share and for a total offering with gross proceeds to the Company of not less than $25 million (a "Qualified IPO").

Company Favorable: The Series [A] Preferred shall be automatically converted into Common Stock, at the then-applicable conversion price, (i) in the event that the holders of at least a majority of the outstanding Series [A] Preferred consent to such conversion or (ii) upon the closing of a firmly underwritten public offering of shares of Common Stock of the Company at a per share price not less than two times the Original Purchase Price (as adjusted for stock splits and the like) and for a total offering of not less than $5 million, before deduction of underwriters commissions and expenses (a "Qualified IPO").

§ 3:11 Dilution clauses

The single most important consideration when raising funds is anticipating how, as a company grows, new rounds of financing will affect the value of the shares of company's existing shareholders. Dilution clauses are the single most important tool for investors who want to ensure that any subsequent financing will, at the very least, not dilute the value of their investments below the price they paid in a prior round. Frothy periods of funding for hi-tech or technology companies can produce some excellent examples of this. During the first wave of fundraising for Internet focused companies in the last 1990's, some companies that were able to raise millions with only a business plan at high pre-money valuations quickly found themselves and their shareholders in a very unhappy position when they went out for subsequent rounds of funding in a bear funding market. Many companies that had actually executed to plan found that they were unable to raise money at higher valuations and, in some cases, had to accept lower pre-money valuations in subsequent rounds than their post-money valuations in prior rounds.

Dilution clauses are important in the event that a company's future financing results in a round of financing at the same price as the previous round, called a flat round, or in a round in which share prices are, when taking dilution into account, lower than the share prices of a previous round, called a down round. The three clauses in Figure 7 stipulate ways of calculating conversion prices in the event that a future share price is dilutive to the investors of the preferred round.

The most Investor Favorable clause implements what is called a full ratchet, which means that the effective cost and ownership percentage in the company for the preferred investor who invested at a given price in a prior round adjusts so that the cost and ownership percentage to the old investor is as if that investor invested in the new round side-by-side. So, if a share price at a Series A Preferred round is $2, and subsequently there is a down round and the share price in a Series B Preferred round is $1, the full ratchet would allow the Preferred A investor to benefit at the time of conversion into common from an adjustment that ensures that the conversion price of his shares is $1, the same conversion price of the new Series B. Because the value per purchase price for Preferred B investors may drop to $1, the conversion price at which that Preferred B investor may convert to common will be set at $1. With a full ratchet, the conversion price at which the Preferred A investor will be allowed to convert his shares will be adjusted in the company charter from $2 to $1, prior to any adjustments for cumulative dividends for example. At that point in time when the Preferred A investor chooses to convert his shares to common, he will convert at a price of $1 instead of $2. The cost for this is to the holders of common stock, whose shares will be the ones to get diluted. Hence the conundrum for companies that are able to receive high pre-money valuations early in the life of a company. The entrepreneur may think that this is a risk worth taking, however valuations that are prematurely high in early rounds can adversely affect the marketability of a company in a later round. Investors who come to the table may sense that the management and its previous investors had lofty and inappropriate expectations and that as a result management may be difficult to work with or to rely on when it comes to future performance. The financial consequences of a down round can also be devastating for existing shareholders whose impatience and soured demeanor can create a less than welcoming environment for new investors.

The Middle of the Road clause results in some dilution for existing preferred shareholders in the event of a future round at a lower price. The clause requires a weighted average conversion which means that the conversion price which is established for an existing class of preferred shares must be changed. The conversion price is simply the price at which the preferred would convert to common. A company's charter will typically state that each share of preferred will convert into the number of shares of common that you get when you divide the preferred price, which in our example above was $2, by the preferred conversion price, which in this case would initially be stated as $2 in the company's charter. In a down-round which effects a weighted average adjustment, the conversion price which is stated in the company's charter must be adjusted and the number of common shares which the preferred is then able to purchase upon conversion is determined by a new conversion price. The following formula on the next page is used to determine the new conversion price for the preferred when a weighted average adjustment is brought into effect:

$$\text{Old Preferred A Conversion Price} \times \frac{\text{\# of Shares of Common Equivalent Outstanding Prior to Preferred B Round} + \text{\# of Shares of Common which amount paid for Preferred B would Purchase if at old Preferred A Conversion Price}}{\text{\# of Shares of Common Equivalent Outstanding Prior to Preferred B Round} + \text{\# of New Shares of Preferred B Issued}}$$

In applying this formula, consider the example used in the full ratchet discussion: a $2 Conversion Price for Preferred A that must be adjusted when a subsequent Preferred B round of 4 million shares is priced at $1 per share. Let us assume that the company had 13 million common equivalent shares outstanding prior to the Preferred B round. Let us also assume that 2 million shares or $4 million had been received from the Preferred A investors in the prior round. Were $4 million to purchase Common at the Conversion Price for the Preferred A as established in the company's charter at the time of the Preferred A round, it would in effect have the buying power to purchase 2 million shares. The resultant weighted average price per share for the Preferred A investor in this scenario would be $1.76 per share; this was derived by applying the formula and our assumptions as follows:

$$\begin{array}{l}\text{Old} \\ \text{Preferred A} \\ \text{Conversion} \\ \text{Price (\$2)}\end{array} \times \frac{\begin{array}{l}\text{\# of Shares of} \\ \text{Common Equiv-} \\ \text{alent outstand-} \\ \text{ing Prior to} \\ \text{Preferred B} \\ \text{Round} \\ \text{(13,000,000)}\end{array} + \begin{array}{l}\text{Common} \\ \text{which} \\ \text{Amount Paid} \\ \text{for Preferred} \\ \text{B would} \\ \text{Purchase if} \\ \text{at old} \\ \text{Preferred A} \\ \text{Conversion} \\ \text{Price} \\ \text{(2,000,000)}\end{array}}{\begin{array}{l}\text{\# of Shares of} \\ \text{Common Equiv-} \\ \text{alent outstand-} \\ \text{ing prior to} \\ \text{Preferred B} \\ \text{Round} \\ \text{(13,000,000)}\end{array} + \begin{array}{l}\text{\# of New} \\ \text{Shares of} \\ \text{Preferred B} \\ \text{issued} \\ \text{(4,000,000)}\end{array}}$$

It is important to note that the Middle of the Road example below includes a "play-or-lose" provision which is not always seen in deals. The provision in this case would require a prior investor to invest his pro-rata share of a subsequent round.

The Company Favorable scenario is one in which there is no dilution protection for the investor. This is typically only seen in first angel rounds, in which all common stocks and stockholders are treated equally.

FIGURE 7

(6) Anti-dilution Provisions:

Investor Favorable: The conversion price of the Series [A] Preferred will be subject to a full ratchet adjustment in the event that the Company issues additional equity securities (other than the reserved employee shares described under "Employee Pool") at a purchase price less than the applicable conversion price. The conversion price will also be subject to proportional adjustment for stock splits, stock dividends, recapitalizations, and the like.

Middle of the Road: The conversion price of the Series [A] Preferred will be then subject to a weighted average adjustment (based on all outstanding shares of Preferred and Common Stock) to reduce dilution in the event that the Company issues additional equity securities (other than the reserved employee shares described under "Employee Pool") at a purchase price less than the applicable conversion price. The conversion price will also be subject to proportional adjustment for stock splits, stock dividends, recapitalizations, and the like. This anti-dilution protection is subject to a play-or-lose provision that provides that adjustments will be made to the Series [A] Conversion Price only if the Series [A] holder participates in such dilutive offering to the extent of its pro rata equity interest in the Preferred. Any investor who does not participate in a future financing forfeits the benefits of dilution protection [for all future rounds of financing/only for that financing round].

Company Favorable: The conversion price of the Series [A] Preferred will be subject to proportional adjustment for stock splits, stock dividends, recapitalizations, and the like.

---

§ 3:12 Voting rights

Voting rights means that in the event that a shareholder vote is called, all shares are treated equally (see Figure 8). It is important to note that there are certain protective provisions that are articulated in Section 8 of this sample term sheet (see Figure 9) that will allow the preferred investor to have powers that do not require the vote of all shareholders. Clearly therefore, voting rights are important to preferred investors, but their level of influence is supplemented by additional powers, examples of which are articulated in Figure 9.

FIGURE 8

---

(7) Voting Rights: [Investor Favorable, Middle of the Road and Company Favorable are the same.]

The Series [A] Preferred will vote together with the Common Stock and not as a separate class except as specifically provided herein or as otherwise required by law. Each share of Series [A] Preferred shall have a number of votes equal to the number of shares of Common Stock then issuable upon conversion of such share of Series [A] Preferred.

---

§ 3:13 Protective provisions

Protective provisions effectively enable the class of shares that are being contemplated to have certain powers associated with them (see Figure 9). Any action taken by the class of shares holding protective provisions would require consent of some proportion of the shareholders of that class. The extent to which these protective provisions are Investor Favorable or Company Favorable will depend upon the type of powers and to what extent the powers are in favor of the investors or the company.

Typically, the concerns that new investors will have, which are often written into the protective provisions section, include whether new shares can be issued with or without the approval of the class of shareholders holding the protective provisions. This means that the preferred shares would, in the case of the Investor Favorable and Middle of the Road examples in Figure 9, like to have an influence and the power to approve any future round of financing that will have a dilutive effect on the value of their securities. In the Investor Favorable example, the preferred will prohibit changes to the rights and preferences associated with the previous stock without majority approval of that class of preferred. The preferred may want to be sure that redemption of common stock by employees who may wish to sell the stock cannot transpire without their approval, and that significant events that would affect the course of the company's business cannot transpire without the approval of that series of preferred. These would include a merger, a reorganization, a sale, amendments to the company's certificate of incorporation, amendments to its bylaws, increases or decreases in the company's number of authorized shares or the size of the board, as well as payments of or the declaration of dividends.

The Middle of the Road example shows powers that are diluted or reduced when compared to the Investor Favorable version. In the Company Favorable example, these powers are virtually eliminated.

The Protective Provisions section is significant in that it articulates and captures the extent to which the investors are expecting to influence certain actions by the company.

FIGURE 9

---

(8) Protective Provisions:

Investor Favorable: The consent of the holders of at least two thirds of the Series [A] Preferred shall be required for any action that (i) alters or changes the rights, preferences, or privileges of the Series [A] Preferred; (ii) increases or decreases the authorized number of shares of Series [A] Preferred; (iii) creates (by reclassification or otherwise) any new class or series of shares having rights, preferences, or privileges senior or pari passu to those of the Series [A] Preferred; (iv) results in the redemption of any shares of Common Stock (other than pursuant to employee agreements); (v) results in any merger, other corporate reorganization, sale of control, or any transaction in which all or substantially all of the assets of the Company are sold or exclusively licensed; (vi) amends or waives any provision of the Company's Certificate of Incorporation or Bylaws; (vii) increases or decreases the authorized size of the Company's board; or (viii) results in the payment or declaration of any dividend on any shares of Common or Preferred Stock.

Middle of the Road: For so long as at least [one-half of the shares originally issued] shares of Series [A] Preferred remain outstanding, consent of the holders of at least two thirds of the Series [A] Preferred shall be required for any action that (i) alters or changes the rights, preferences, or privileges of the Series [A] Preferred; (ii) increases or decreases the authorized number of shares of Common or Preferred Stock; (iii) creates (by reclassification or otherwise) any new class or series of shares having rights, preferences, or privileges senior to or pari passu with the Series [A] Preferred; (iv) results in the redemption of any shares of Common Stock (other than pursuant to equity incentive agreements with service providers giving the Company the right to repurchase shares upon the termination of services); (v) results in any merger, other corporate reorganization, sale of control, or any transaction in which all or substantially all of the assets of the Company are sold; or (vi) amends or waives any provision of the Company's Certificate of Incorporation or Bylaws relative to the Series [A] Preferred.

Company Favorable: The consent of the holders of at least 50 percent of the Series [A] Preferred shall be required for any action that (i) adversely alters or changes the rights, preferences, or privileges of the Series [A] Preferred, or (ii) decreases the authorized number of shares of Series [A] Preferred.

---

§ 3:14 Board composition

The language of any Board Composition and Meetings section is typically straightforward. But the board composition that is proposed will typically contemplate an effective change in the influence, balance, and role of the board as a result of the addition of or substitution of board representation of the investors proposing the term sheet. Investor Favorable clauses will typically propose a board composition that will give the class of shares created as a result of the contemplated investment a majority control directly or indirectly on the board of the company. A Middle of the Road scenario would perhaps contemplate an odd-numbered board that proposes an equal number of seats to the common or the management of the company, an equal number to the preferred stock or venture investors, and one independent who is mutually agreed upon.

The Company Favorable scenario below is favorable to the company because on an as-converted basis, the founders and their friends and family would own enough common stock to ensure a majority vote on a shareholder-vote basis to support the profile of a board that the founders and management would prefer.

FIGURE 10

---

(9) Board Composition and Meetings:
Investor Favorable: The size of the Company's Board of Directors shall initially be set at [three]. The holders of the Series [A] preferred, voting as a separate class, shall be entitled to elect two members of the Company's Board of Directors, the holders of the Common Stock shall be entitled to elect one member, and the third member shall be mutually agreed upon. The Board shall initially be composed of [_______], [________________], and [__________________]. Board of Directors will be elected annually. Board of Directors meetings will be held at least four times per year. Until the Company is profitable or the Board otherwise agrees, Board meetings will be targeted for every two months, or six times per year.

Middle of the Road: The size of the Company's Board of Directors shall be set at [five]. The Board shall initially be composed of [_______], [__________________], [__________________], [__________________], and [________________]. At each meeting for the election of directors, the holders of the Series [A] Preferred, voting as a separate class, shall be entitled to elect one member of the Company's Board of Directors, the holders of Common Stock, voting as a separate class, shall be entitled to elect two members, and the remaining directors will be mutually agreed upon by the Common and Preferred. It is anticipated that the Company's CEO will occupy one of the remaining seats. Board of Directors meetings will be held at least four times per year. Until the Company is profitable or the Board otherwise agrees, Board meetings will be targeted for every two months, or six times per year.

Company Favorable: The size of the Company's Board of Directors shall initially be set at [five]. All directors shall be elected by the shareholders voting on an as-converted basis.

---

§ 3:15 Special board approval items

The Special Board Approval Items section is a rider that

may or may not be included in a term sheet; it is entirely negotiable (see Figure 11). But it is a critical section to understand, because some of these issues may represent issues of control, such as a requirement that the board provide approval for hiring of officers of the company or senior management or for the assumption of debt by the company above certain prescribed levels that have not previously been articulated in the company's articles of incorporation or bylaws.

FIGURE 11

---

(10) Special Board Approval Items:

Board approval will be required for:

1. Hiring of all officers of the Company.
2. Any employment agreements (approval by a majority of disinterested Directors, or a Compensation Committee when established).
3. Compensation programs including base salaries and bonus programs for all officers and key employees (approval by a majority of disinterested Directors or a Compensation Committee when established).
4. All stock option programs as well as issuance of all stock and stock options (approval by a majority of disinterested Directors or a Compensation Committee when established).
5. Annual budgets, business plans, and financial plans.
6. All real estate leases or purchases.
7. Execution of entrance obligations or commitments, including capital equipment leases or purchases, with total value greater than $[________] and which are outside the most recent business plan or budget approved by the Board of Directors.

---

§ 3:16 Information rights

Information rights define the extent to which investors are given access to information in a company (see Figure 12). The most complete and Investor Favorable type of investors rights are typically referred to by the term forensic audit: An investor requires that he be able to examine almost any document, audited or unaudited, financial or otherwise, that may exist in a company's files or accounting software. A Middle of the Road scenario is clearly less Investor Favorable and dilutes the power or the type of demands that can be made by the investors in terms of access to information. A Company Favorable scenario limits the amount of information that it is required to provide to investors. The extent to which entrepreneurs push back on the language proposed in the Information Rights section will reveal the extent to which they may be control-oriented by nature or have something to hide.

One important area to examine in the Information Rights section is whether the requirements that are articulated may be unique to a specific firm; a firm may require from all of its investments the type of rights proposed. These requests may not signal the attitude of the firm, but some of its past experiences. In the case of asking for forensic audit rights, for example, an investor may have been burned in the past and now requires the ability to closely examine the books of their invested entities.

Whether this transpires is another issue. It may be that unless the investor suspects fraud or other questionable activities, specific types of information are never actually requested. Nevertheless, information rights can be a disruptive and concerning clause, unless the entrepreneur explores the investor's background and rationale for including it.

It is also not uncommon for an investor to require observer rights, which is the ability to sit in on board meetings and have access to information at the board level. It does not allow them the rights to vote; however entrepreneurs should not be naive. Observers can have significant voice and influence in the mood and tenor of board discussions. Particularly with strategic investors, who can glean levels of information that otherwise might not be shared in as timely and open a fashion with all investors.

FIGURE 12

---

(11) Information Rights:

Investor Favorable: So long as an Investor continues to

hold shares of Series [A] Preferred or Common Stock issued upon conversion of the Series [A] Preferred, the Company shall deliver to the Investor audited annual financial statements, audited by a Big Five accounting firm, and unaudited quarterly financial statements. In addition, the Company will furnish the Investor with monthly and quarterly financial statements and will provide a copy of the Company's annual operating plan within 30 days prior to the beginning of the fiscal year. Each Investor shall also be entitled to standard inspection and visitation rights.

Middle of the Road: So long as an Investor continues to hold shares of Series [A] Preferred or Common Stock issued upon conversion of the Series [A] Preferred, the Company shall deliver to the Investor audited annual financial statements audited by a Big Five accounting firm and unaudited quarterly financial statements. So long as an Investor holds not less than [one quarter of the Shares originally issued] shares of Series [A] Preferred (or [one quarter of the Shares originally issued] shares of the Common Stock issued upon conversion of the Series [A] Preferred, or a combination of both), the Company will furnish the Investor with monthly financial statements compared against plan and will provide a copy of the Company's annual operating plan within 30 days prior to the beginning of the fiscal year. Each Investor shall also be entitled to standard inspection and visitation rights. These provisions shall terminate upon a public offering of the Company's Common Stock.

Company Favorable: So long as an Investor continues to hold shares of Series [A] Preferred or Common Stock issued upon conversion of the Series [A] Preferred, the Company shall deliver to the Investor audited annual financial statements audited by a Big Five accounting firm and unaudited quarterly financial statements. Each Investor shall also be entitled to standard inspection and visitation rights. These provisions shall terminate upon a registered public offering of the Company's Common Stock.

---

§ 3:17 Registration rights

The registration rights section stipulates the extent to which preferred versus common stock will share equal or preferential treatment when their securities have been converted and are participating in a public offering or registration subsequent to a public offering (see Figure 13). This will depend upon whether the registration rights section is Investor or Company Favorable. The extent to which the Registration Rights language of a term sheet stands up at the time of a contemplated IPO will be more a function of the influence of the investor at the time of the public offering, the nature of the financial markets at the time of the offering, and the strength of the underwriter's influence at that time.

The weight and influences of these clauses can vary significantly depending upon the timing and context of public offerings. It is possible that in the excitement of the public offering an underwriter, depending upon the underwriter's weight and influence in the public markets, may require significant changes to the manner in which these clauses are treated at the time of an actual offering and thereafter. So, depending upon the situation at the time of an offering, the underwriter's influence may be such that some of the language contemplated in this section and later incorporated in the company's articles of incorporation or charter may be revisited.

The variables here are the number of registrations that the company is obligated to effect, the period of time in which these registrations are required, and the economic cost of going through registration.

FIGURE 13

---

(12) Registration Rights:

Investor Favorable: Demand Rights: If Investors holding at least 30 percent of the outstanding shares of Series [A] Preferred, including Common Stock issued on conversion of Series [A] Preferred ("Registrable Securities"), request that the Company file a Registration Statement having an aggregate offering price to the public of not less than $5,000,000, the Company will use its best efforts to cause such shares to be registered; provided, however, that the Company shall not be obligated to effect any such registration prior to the second anniversary of the Closing. The Company shall have the right to delay such registration under certain circumstances for two periods not in excess of ninety (90) days each in any twelve (12) month period.

The Company shall not be obligated to effect more than two (2) registrations under these demand right provisions, and shall not be obligated to effect a registration (i) during the ninety (90) day period commencing with the date of the Company's initial public offering, or (ii) if it delivers notice to the holders of the Registrable Securities within thirty (30) days of any registration request of its intent to file a registration statement for a Qualified IPO within ninety (90) days.

Company Registration: The Investors shall be entitled to "piggy-back" registration rights on all registrations of the Company or on any demand registrations of any other investor subject to the right, however, of the Company and its underwriters to reduce the number of shares proposed to be registered pro rata in view of market conditions. If the Investors are so limited, however, no party shall sell shares in such registration other than the Company or the Investor, if any, invoking the demand registration. No shareholder of the Company shall be granted piggy-back registration rights that would reduce the number of shares includable by the holders of the Registrable Securities in such registration without the consent of the holders of at least two thirds of the Registrable Securities.

S-3 Rights: Investors shall be entitled to an unlimited number of demand registrations on Form S-3 (if available to the Company) so long as such registered offerings are not less than $500,000. The Company shall not be obligated to file more than one S-3 registration in any six month period.

Expenses: The Company shall bear registration expenses (exclusive of underwriting discounts and commissions) of all such demands, piggy-backs, and S-3 registrations (including the expense of one special counsel of the selling shareholders).

Transfer of Rights: The registration rights may be transferred to (i) any partner or retired partner of any holder which is a partnership, (ii) any family member or trust for the benefit of any individual holder, or (iii) any transferee who acquires at least [one quarter of the shares originally issued] shares of Registrable Securities; provided the Company is given written notice thereof.

Standoff Provision: No Investor holding more than 1 percent of the Company will sell shares within 120 days of the effective date of the Company's initial public offering if all officers, directors, and other 1 percent shareholders are similarly bound.

Other Provisions: Other provisions shall be contained in the Investor Rights Agreement with respect to registration rights as are reasonable, including cross-indemnification, the period of time in which the Registration Statement shall be kept effective, and underwriting arrangements.

Middle of the Road: Demand Rights: If Investors holding more than 50 percent of the outstanding shares of Series [A] Preferred, including Common Stock issued on conversion of Series [A] Preferred ("Registrable Securities"), request that the Company file a Registration Statement having an aggregate offering price to the public of not less than $5,000,000, the Company will use its best efforts to cause such shares to be registered; provided, however, that the Company shall not be obligated to effect any such registration prior to the third anniversary of the Closing. The Company shall have the right to delay such registration under certain circumstances for one period not in excess of ninety (90) days in any twelve (12) month period.

The Company shall not be obligated to effect more than two (2) registrations under these demand right provisions, and shall not be obligated to effect a registration (i) during the one hundred eighty (180) day period commencing with the date of the Company's initial public offering, or (ii) if it delivers notice to the holders of the Registrable Securities within thirty (30) days of any registration request of its intent to file a registration statement for such initial public offering within ninety (90) days.

Company Registration: The Investors shall be entitled to "piggy-back" registration rights on all registrations of the Company or on any demand registrations of any other investor subject to the right, however, of the Company and its underwriters to reduce the number of shares proposed to be registered pro rata in view of market conditions. If the Investors are so limited, however, no party shall sell shares in such registration other than the Company or the Investor, if any, invoking the demand registration. No shareholder of the Company shall be granted piggy-back registration rights that would reduce the number of shares includable by the holders of the Registrable Securities in such registration without the consent of the holders of at least two thirds of the Registrable Securities.

S-3 Rights: Investors shall be entitled to two (2) demand registrations on Form S-3 (if available to the Company) so long as such registered offerings are not less than $500,000.

Expenses: The Company shall bear registration expenses (exclusive of underwriting discounts and commissions) of all such demands, piggy-backs, and S-3 registrations (including the expense of one special counsel of the selling shareholders not to exceed $15,000).

Transfer of Rights: The registration rights may be transferred to (i) any partner or retired partner of any holder which is a partnership, (ii) any family member or trust for the benefit of any individual holder, or (iii) any transferee who acquires at least [one eighth of the shares originally issued] shares of Registrable Securities; provided the Company is given written notice thereof.

Lock-Up Provision: If requested by the Company and its underwriters, no Investor will sell its shares for a specified period (but not to exceed 180 days) following the effective date of the Company's initial public offering; provided that all officers, directors, and other 1 percent shareholders are similarly bound.

Other Provisions: Other provisions shall be contained in the Investor Rights Agreement with respect to registration rights as are reasonable, including cross-indemnification, the period of time in which the Registration Statement shall be kept effective, and underwriting arrangements.

Company Favorable: Company Registration: The Investors shall be entitled to "piggy-back" registration rights on all registrations of the Company subject to the right, however, of the Company and its underwriters to reduce the number of shares proposed to be registered pro rata among all Investors in view of market conditions.

S-3 Rights: Investors shall be entitled to two (2) demand registrations on Form S-3 (if available to the Company) so long as such registered offerings are not less than $500,000.

Expenses: The Company shall bear registration expenses (exclusive of underwriting discounts and commissions) of all such piggy-backs, and S-3 registrations (including the expense of a single counsel to the selling shareholders not to exceed $5,000).

Standoff Provision: If requested by the underwriters no Investor will sell shares of the Company's stock for up to 180 days following a public offering by the Company of its stock.

Termination of Rights: The registration rights shall terminate on the date three (3) years after the Company's initial public offering, or with respect to each Investor, at such time as (i) the Company's shares are publicly traded, and (ii) the Investor is entitled to sell all of its shares in any ninety (90) day period pursuant to SEC Rule 144.

Other Provisions: Other provisions shall be contained in the Investor Rights Agreement with respect to registration rights as are reasonable and standard, including cross-indemnification, the period of time in which the Registration Statement shall be kept effective, and underwriting arrangements.

§ 3:18 Right of first refusal

The Right of First Refusal is a clause that investors include to ensure that an investor is able to have influence over the sale of any shares, be they preferred or common, and to retain the ability to either purchase those shares or restrict their sale (see Figure 14). The degree to which these are Company or Investor Favorable is a function of the amount of influence the company has over an investor's right to refuse a sale.

FIGURE 14

(13) Right of First Refusal:
Investor Favorable: The Investors shall have the right in the event the Company proposes to offer equity securities to any person (other than securities issued pursuant to employee benefit plans or acquisitions, in each case as approved by the Board of Directors, including the director elected by holders of the Series [A] Preferred) to purchase on a pro rata basis all or any portion of such shares. Any securities not subscribed for by an Investor may be reallocated among the other Investors. If the Investors do not purchase all of such securities, that portion that is not purchased may be offered to other parties on terms no less favorable to the Company for a period of sixty (60) days. Such right of first refusal will terminate upon a Qualified IPO.

Middle of the Road: Investors holding at least [one eighth of the shares originally issued] shares of Registrable Securities shall have the right in the event the Company proposes to offer equity securities to any person (other than securities issued pursuant to employee benefit plans or pursuant to acquisitions) to purchase their pro rata portion of such shares. Any securities not subscribed for by an eligible Investor may be reallocated among the other eligible Investors. Such right of first refusal will terminate upon a Qualified IPO.

Company Favorable: Each Investor holding at least [one quarter of the shares originally issued] shares of Series [A] Preferred shall have the right in the event the Company proposes to offer equity securities to any person (other than securities issued to employees, directors, or consultants or pursuant to acquisitions, etc.) to purchase its pro rata share of such securities (based on the total fully diluted number of common stock equivalents outstanding). Such right of first refusal will terminate upon an underwritten public offering of shares of the Company.

---

§ 3:19 Conditions precedent

The Conditions Precedent section in many ways presents a road map to the completion of the financing that is proposed by the term sheet (see Figure 15).

It details the due diligence that must be completed once the term sheet has been agreed upon and highlights that a round of financing will not be complete until the final purchase and sale agreement has been signed by prospective investors, any amendments to the articles of incorporation that may be necessary have been made, and the money is in the bank.

This section is provided more for education purposes, because it is often not included in its entirety in term sheets. A company, in contemplating and agreeing to a term sheet, should be expecting to do whatever it takes to accommodate the investors' due diligence.

FIGURE 15

---

(14) Conditions Precedent:

Investor Favorable: This proposal is non-binding, and is specifically subject to:

(1) Completed due-diligence reviews satisfactory to [Investor] and Investors' counsel, specifically including review of [Investor Counsel].

(2) Customary stock purchase and related agreements satisfactory to [Investor] and Investors' counsel, including stock option plan.

(3) Intellectual property, confidentiality, and non-compete agreements with all key employees of the Company satisfactory to Investors' counsel.
(4) Satisfactory review of the Company's compensation programs and stock allocation and vesting arrangements for officers, key employees, and others, as well as any existing employment or similar agreements.
(5) Both the Company and Investors will negotiate exclusively and in good faith toward an investment as outlined in this proposal and agree to "no-shop" provisions for reasonable and customary periods of time.
(6) Conversion of all outstanding convertible securities (e.g., convertible notes or preferred stock issued prior to the date of this Series A financing).

Middle of the Road and Company Favorable: This proposal is non-binding, and is specifically subject to:
(1) Completed due-diligence reviews satisfactory to [Investor] and Investors' counsel, specifically including review of [Investor Counsel].
(2) Customary stock purchase and related agreements satisfactory to [Investor] and Investors' counsel, including stock option plan.
(3) Both the Company and Investors will negotiate exclusively and in good faith toward an investment as outlined in this proposal and agree to "no-shop" provisions for reasonable and customary periods of time.

---

§ 3:20 Purchase agreement

The Purchase Agreement is the document that investors sign in order to purchase shares in a company. The major difference between the Investor Favorable and Middle of the Road passages in Figure 16 is the requirement in the Investor Favorable section that the founders make certain representations. The extent to which the founders warrant certain items provides investors both with more comfort and with an additional tool that enables them to have legal recourse against a founder in the event that such representations prove to be inaccurate after a financing. The Company Favorable passage in this example not only excludes the requirement for representations by the founders but lowers the bar with respect to the percentage of the class of stock that must approve any amendment to the stockholder's agreement. Often a series of stock will be purchased by multiple parties, so the lower the percentage required to make an amendment to the stockholder's agreement the greater the flexibility of the company going forward.

Once a term sheet has been accepted, a company and its counsel will be expected to produce certain legal and other documentation. The first item will be a Purchase Agreement, which provides for the purchase of the form of security that is being contemplated in the term sheet. The second will be the form of the Investment Security, which details the terms and conditions of the actual security that the investor purchases. It will describe the liquidation rights, voting rights, dividends, etc. that are provided to the venture investor. The third is a Registration Rights Agreement that provides the venture investor with the right to force registration of the securities held, under the Securities Act and other applicable laws. The fourth is a Stockholder's Agreement, which is entered into among the company, the founders, and the firm. This agreement refers to and relates to the governance of the company and any sales of the securities by the company's management or current stockholders.

FIGURE 16

---

(15) Purchase Agreement:

Investor Favorable: The investment shall be made pursuant to a Stock Purchase Agreement reasonably acceptable to the Company and the Investors, which agreement shall contain, among other things, appropriate representations and warranties of the Company, representations of the Founders with respect to patents, litigation, previous employment and outside activities, covenants of the Company reflecting the provisions set forth herein, and appropriate conditions of closing, including an opinion of counsel for the Company. The Stock Purchase Agreement shall provide that it may only be amended and any waivers thereunder shall only be made with the approval of the holders of two thirds of the Series [A] Preferred.

Registration rights provisions may be amended or waived solely with the consent of the holders of two thirds of the Registrable Securities.

Middle of the Road: The investment shall be made pursuant to a Stock Purchase Agreement reasonably acceptable to the Company and the Investors, which agreement shall contain, among other things, appropriate representations and warranties of the Company, covenants of the Company reflecting the provisions set forth herein, and appropriate conditions of closing, including an opinion of counsel for the Company. The Stock Purchase Agreement shall provide that it may only be amended and any waivers thereunder shall only be made with the approval of the holders of two thirds of the Series [A] Preferred. Registration rights provisions may be amended or waived solely with the consent of the holders of two thirds of the Registrable Securities.

Company Favorable: The investment shall be made pursuant to a Stock Purchase Agreement reasonably acceptable to the Company and the Investors, which agreement shall contain, among other things, appropriate representations and warranties of the Company, covenants of the Company reflecting the provisions set forth herein, and appropriate conditions of closing, including an opinion of counsel for the Company. The Stock Purchase Agreement shall provide that it may only be amended and any waivers thereunder shall only be made with the approval of the holders of 50 percent of the Series [A] Preferred. Registration rights provisions may be amended or waived solely with the consent of the holders of 50 percent of the Registrable Securities.

---

§ 3:21 Employee matters

Anyone involved in a financing, whether as employees or investors, put a high value on flexibility and liquidity. The terms articulated in the Employee Matters section, examples of which are contained in Figure 17, will typically outline the number of shares of common stock reserved for options pools and specific investing programs, co-sale agreements, whether key management insurance will be provided for key employees, and any management hires that may transpire subsequent to the financing. From an investor's perspective, the language in this section will strive to put some reigns on some of the powers employees and founders may have with regard to their stock in the company.

When asked what the most important thing is about a deal, investors will typically say Management, Management, Management. And so, for example, affording key employees and founders the ability to cash out of their shares in advance of later stage investors is typically restricted; the Employee Matters section is where the nature of these restrictions will be articulated. This makes sense if one assumes that the future value of a company is directly related to the motivation and performance of founders and management. It stands to reason that if this class of stakeholder cashes out early in the game, the company could be left in a position where it needs to both refresh its options pools and attract more incentivized management. It is not uncommon, therefore, that investors will also require Key Man insurance in order to provide the company with a buffer in the event that a founder or series of key employees die.

The degrees to which the examples of text included are Investor or Company Favorable are really a matter of how tightly the clauses are drafted and how flexible or restrictive they are. Often in the early stages of a company, at the urging of sophisticated angel investors who are buying common stock or when the first round of preferred stock is being contemplated by a venture investor, these issues will be discussed and incorporated into the company's bylaws in great detail. Once established, there may be little need in later rounds to amend these terms or incorporate them into a term sheet.

The section may articulate, for example, whether future options, if issued, will be issued and if so for whom they will be dilutive. A term sheet may require that additional options be issued on a pre-money basis, therefore only diluting existing investors and not the new investors. There may, however, be some unissued options in an existing pool, in which case new investors are likely to agree that the financing assumes that any future number of options, up to some specific number, will be equally dilutive to current and new shareholders.

Typically, the price of a share that is incorporated in the term sheet reflects the expectations of the new investor as to how options will be treated. And these expectations may be further detailed in the Employee Matters section. Often a new investor assumes that a board would determine rationally and reasonably how options would be issued should a policy already have been put in place with regard to issuance of options.

FIGURE 17

---

(16) Employee Matters:

Investor Favorable:

Employee Pool: Upon the Closing of this financing there will be [____] shares of issued and outstanding Common Stock held by the Founders and an additional [____] shares of Common Stock reserved for future issuance to key employees.

Stock Vesting: All stock and stock equivalents issued after the Closing to employees, directors and consultants will be subject to vesting as follows: 20 percent to vest at the end of the first year following such issuance, with the remaining 80 percent to vest monthly over the subsequent four years. The repurchase option shall provide that upon termination of the employment of the shareholder, with or without cause, the Company or its assignee (to the extent permissible under applicable securities law qualification) retains the option to repurchase at cost any unvested shares held by such shareholder.

Common Stock currently held by the Founders will be subject to similar vesting terms, with such vesting period beginning as of the Closing Date.

Restrictions on Sales: The Company shall have a right of first refusal on all transfers of Common Stock.

Proprietary Information and Inventions

Agreement: Each officer, employee and consultant of the Company shall enter into an acceptable proprietary information and inventions agreement.

Co-Sale Agreement: The shares of the Company's securities held by the Founders of the Company shall be made subject to a co-sale agreement (with certain reasonable exceptions) with the holders of the Series [A] Preferred such that the Founders may not sell, transfer or exchange their stock unless each holder of Series [A] Preferred has an opportunity to participate in the sale on a pro rata basis. This right of co-sale shall not apply to and shall terminate upon a Qualified IPO.

Key-Man Insurance: As soon as reasonably possible after the Closing, the Company shall procure a key-man life insurance policy for [________] in the amount of $1,000,000, naming the Company as beneficiary; provided, however, that at the election of holders of a majority of the outstanding Series [A] Preferred, such proceeds shall be used to redeem shares of Series [A] Preferred.

Management: The Company will, on a best efforts basis, hire a chief [________] officer within the six (6) month period following the closing of the financing.

Middle of the Road:

Employee Pool: Upon the Closing of this financing there will be [____] shares of issued and outstanding Common Stock held by the Founders and an additional [____] shares of Common Stock reserved for future issuance to key employees. Promptly after the Closing, Messrs. [________] and [________] will be granted incentive stock options from the [________] share pool in the amount of [________] shares each exercisable at $0.10 per share, which options will vest in accordance with the following paragraph.

Stock Vesting: All stock and stock equivalents issued after the Closing to employees, directors, consultants and other service providers will be subject to vesting as follows: [20 percent to vest at the end of the first year following such issuance, with the remaining 80 percent to vest monthly over the next four years.] The repurchase option shall provide that upon termination of the employment of the shareholder, with or without cause, the Company or its assignee (to the extent permissible under applicable securities law qualification) retains the option to repurchase at cost any unvested shares held by such shareholder.

The outstanding Common Stock currently held by the Founders will be subject to similar vesting terms, provided that the Founders shall be credited with two years of vesting as of the Closing, with their remaining unvested shares to vest monthly over three years.

Restrictions on Sales: The Company shall have a right of first refusal on all transfers of Common Stock, subject to normal exceptions.

Proprietary Information and Inventions

Agreement: Each officer and employee of the Company shall enter into an acceptable proprietary information and inventions agreement.

Co-Sale Agreement: The shares of the Company's securities held by [____________________], [____________________], [____________________] and [________] (the "Founders") shall be made subject to a co-sale agreement (with certain reasonable exceptions) with the holders of the Series [A] Preferred such that the Founders may not sell, transfer or exchange their stock unless each holder of Series [A] Preferred has an opportunity to participate in the sale on a pro rata basis. This right of co-sale shall not apply to and shall terminate upon the Company's initial public offering.

Key-Man Insurance: The Company shall procure a key-man life insurance policy for [________] in the amount of $1,000,000, naming the Company as beneficiary.

Company Favorable: None.

---

§ 3:22 Closing date, legal counsel, expenses, and finders

These four sections, as detailed in Figure 18, can have a significant influence over the outcome of a closing and the economics of a deal.

The closing date needs to be realistic. Entrepreneurs should consult existing investors or other sources of capital on what is an optimal closing date. This is to ensure that in the event that the closing process, including drafting of legal documents, takes longer than expected the entrepreneur does not put undue pressure on a new investor or group of investors to work more quickly than is realistic.

More important is the choice of legal counsel. Entrepreneurs should not underestimate this. If a company offers a second or subsequent round of preferred stock, it may be appropriate for the company's counsel to draft the documents for the subsequent round, if the new and current investors are reasonably satisfied with the format and quality of the documentation for the prior round of preferred stock.

If the investors are offering to purchase a first round of preferred stock, Series A, or feel strongly about leading the drafting process, it would be reasonable to let the investor's counsel take the lead. In this case it would also be advisable to ensure that company's counsel is experienced in the type of transaction contemplated. If the company's counsel is tasked with the drafting, counsel to the new round of investors is likely to be very involved. The counsel to the new investor or to the lead for a syndicate of investors will want to be actively involved in reviewing and proposing changes to any documentation that company's counsel produces.

If the entrepreneur had a bad experience with company counsel in drafting a previous round of documents, changing legal counsel would be a smart idea. Many venture investors have typically worked with their counsel on a number of deals and will understandably have a short fuse if company's counsel is inexperienced or does not consider the company's account a priority.

There may be a number of firms or parties involved in financing, and each may have their own attorneys, but the round should be looking to one legal counsel in particular to represent the investors.

Expenses can mount up when multiple law firms are involved. The reality is that if the company prefers to have its own counsel draft documents, the lead investor's counsel will try to eliminate duplication of work but will to an extent be spending an equal amount of time reviewing and proposing changes to documentation produced by company's counsel. Entrepreneurs must remember that most venture investors expect that the expenses of counsel to the lead investor will be borne by the company as a consequence of the contemplated financing. Being too hard-nosed about accommodating a reasonable amount of expenses on the part of the lead can be mistake.

Finally, the Finders clause details how finder's fees will be handled. In the example below, the company and the investor are agreeing to indemnify each other for finder's fees that may eventualize. Unless a deal is very competitive, it is common for an investor to look to the company to cover expenses related to a finder who introduced a deal to the investor.

FIGURE 18

Closing Date: [________], 200[________________________] (the "Closing Date").

Legal Counsel: The Company shall select legal counsel acceptable to [Investor] ([________]). Unless counsels agree otherwise, Investors' counsel [________] shall draft the financing documents for review by Company counsel.

Expenses:

Investor Favorable: The Company shall pay the reasonable fees and expenses of Investors' counsel and Company counsel.

Middle of the Road: The Company shall pay the reasonable

fees for one special counsel to the Investors, expected not to exceed $[25,000 – $35,000], and for Company counsel.

Company Favorable: The Company and the Investors shall each bear their own legal fees and expenses in connection with the transaction.

Finders: The Company and the Investors shall each indemnify the other for any finder's fees for which either is responsible.

Chapter 4

Valuations and the Term Sheet

§ 4:1 Determining value

The price a significant investor is willing to pay for a company on a per share basis determines the value on a per share basis of each of the shares of the company. The reason term sheets are given such serious consideration is that typically there are a host of attendant conditions that new investors wish to attach to the new classes of shares that are offered in each successive financing in the life of a company. While a company's valuation is simply a function of the price the investor is willing to pay, imbedded in the valuation are a host of assumptions and expectations of investors that may or may not be shared by the company. Herein lies the root of the differences that may arise between the valuations proposed by investors and those expected or ultimately accepted by a company.

When an entrepreneur is considering the amount of investment contemplated by an investor or group of investors, as well as the percentage of the company that the investor(s) will purchase and the price offered per share, he should consider three critical issues. First, the value of any company is often the sum of several parts. An investor may discount the revenue stream or earnings of one or several parts of a business and assign different values to different parts of the business.

Second, the entrepreneur should consider carefully the effect that any future financing plans or contingent financing plans may have on the future value of the company and that are likely to be open to interpretation and a point of disagreement for the company and its investors. Failing to anticipate future capital needs when agreeing to a share price for a round of financing can be fatal. A company that is overpriced today or that appears fairly priced but under-performs and requires a subsequent, unanticipated round of financing will be met with suspicion by future investors and likely be penalized, to the disappointment of current investors. The question to ask is, where is the valuation going to take the company? This is as true in public company shares as it is in venture-backed private companies.

Third, there is embedded in the value of a share an expectation that the price for which a share is offered today is at a discount to some future value. Even if the entrepreneur and a prospective investor see eye to eye on future financing needs and the likely revenue numbers and earnings figures for a company going forward, the likely value for which a company can be sold or go public at some future point in time is open to interpretation. The more adept and informed an entrepreneur is in selecting and comparing appropriate comparables and considering the possible effects of depressed markets on future valuations of those comparables, the more likely his expectations with regard to future valuations will be tempered and closer to those of investors.

The mechanics of how pre-money and post-money valuations can be calculated are discussed in the Post-Financing Capitalization section of Chapter 3.

§ 4:2 Creating return on investment

The quantitative and qualitative factors that influence how a venture investor determines the pre-money valuation of a share are as much a function of the investor's internal hurdles and requirements for a return as they are a result of his view of what the likely scenario is for a liquidity event and in what time frame. The expected investment returns by different types of investors and their internal hurdles will vary, so the valuations offered to companies will of course vary.

Venture funds and their investors will usually have clear expectations with respect to returns; these typically boil down to an expectation that investments will generate certain minimum multiples on investment and hence minimum rates of return. The returns for a venture fund are a function of fees charged investors and returns generated from investments. A fund with $100 million in committed capital will typically charge an annual fee of 2 percent, which over a 10 year period equates to $20 million in fee expenses. Simplistically speaking, a venture investor with a $100 million fund has $250,000 in overhead expense associated with every $1 million the fund actually invests. Therefore, a $1 million investment that yields a multiple of two times actually only yields a net multiple of 1.75 times. The longer an investment is under management the greater the spread between the gross return and net return on an investment. Time value of money weighs heavily in a venture investor's calculations. And not every investment does well; a core of investments will excel, a second group might do one to two times the initial investment, and the balance are write-offs. An investment that yields a multiple on original investment of five times invested capital in four years would generate the equivalent internal rate of return (IRR) of 49 percent; the same investment could produce a return for the investor of only 2.25 times original investment in two years and yield roughly the same IRR. Because of the relatively high cost of capital for venture investors, often internal hurdles for gross IRR returns will be 50 percent or more. This translates to net returns in the mid-30s for investors.

How appropriate an investor's valuation is depends not only upon the stage of the investment and the investor's internal hurdles, but upon the extent to which the business is predictable and a thorough evaluation of the different parts and prospects for a company's business is possible. In the very early stages in the life of a company expectations tend to be more tempered, at a time when valuations can often over or under estimate upside or downside, for the simple reason that business models and plans change dramatically in earlier stage companies. Early stage companies often learn as they go and that can either be at the expense of investors or can result in some pleasant surprises. Later stage valuations tend to be more a function of short- to near-term exit expectations, which are tightly tied to expectations about the public markets and known comparables in public markets or to a range of examples of purchase prices by likely and known potential strategic acquirers.

For some, the term strategic investor connotes investors with lower hurdles and an ability to offer rich valuations. There is truth to the fact that strategic investors will sometimes overpay when compared to venture investors, but they typically will only do so when they are acquiring proprietary access to technology or other benefits like the opportunity to develop a sales channel. It is, however, more likely that strategic investors will look to experienced venture investors to lead a round and will participate in a syndicate for strategic as well as financial reasons. The nature of the relationship that develops between portfolio company and strategic investor clearly takes on a symbiotic nature in the best of situations.

Typically, the central concern and focus for an entrepreneur when reviewing and agreeing to a valuation is how that valuation and any associated terms in the term sheet may dilute the entrepreneur. Management should not lose sight of the opportunity to earn additional awards in the form of options by proposing aggressive and achievable revenue plans that accelerate revenue growth and thereby stand to increase the value pie. Venture investors will typically be motivated to consider additional awards in the form of options if they are tied to more aggressive growth and yield a chance at achieving liquidity earlier.

§ 4:3 How to conduct a valuation

There are a variety of ways to determine the current value of a company. The most important task for an investor is to project the likely value for a company at the time at which the company may generate liquidity for the investor, either by being sold or by going public, and then to discount that future value to the present based on a rate of return that is preferred by the investor.

Assume, for example, that a group of preferred investors expect that a media company can be sold for $150 million in four years. The investors have agreed with management that the company is likely to generate $60 million in revenues in four years and project a valuation of $150 million at time of exit. This is based on two factors: 1) according to data from Standard & Poors, the average price for buy-outs of media companies with revenues of between $100 million and $250 million have been roughly 2.5 times revenues or 8.5 times Earnings Before Interest Taxes Depreciation and Amortization (EBITDA); 2) the investors are fairly confident that management has the capability to generate EBITDA of $18 million in year four and revenues of $60 million, so the future valuation at time of exit makes sense.

Now assume that the company is valued at $20 million post-money today and that the investors own 25 percent of the company today based on their initial investment of $5 million. Also assume that in 24 months the company is going to have to raise an additional $10 million of expansion capital in order to grow the business to a point where it will have $60 million in revenues at the end of four years. The venture investor must first determine the company's value in two years. If the company has, say, $25 million in revenues at that time, it is conceivable that the company may be valued at $50 million pre-money. This again is based on the investor's expectations that if the company raises $10 million in new money and the company generates $60 million in revenues in year four, the company will be worth 2.5 times revenue or $150 million.

Assuming that the original investors do not participate in the second round, their ownership percentage would have dropped from 25 percent to 21 percent. After four years the investors' $5 million investment would, based on these assumptions, potentially be worth $31.5 million. This would represent a multiple of 6.3 times or a gross IRR of roughly 58 percent over four years.

§ 4:4 Analyzing a future exit

When a venture firm wants to create a valuation based on a future exit, it considers current value as a function of the likely outcomes for possible exit values and times. The extent to which comparables are reliable and available in the public and private markets is clearly important in guiding investors. So, for example, if investors are looking at a pure services company, they might consider companies like Service Master, and consider the multiples at which those companies are trading. In choosing appropriate comparables, one must first consider what that company's growth rates are and whether the comparison is appropriate. Service Master is a multibillion-dollar company and may not be an appropriate comparable for a company that is expected to have $100 million in revenues in a matter of years.

Basically, the investor is looking for comparables in the public and private market with similar business models and in sectors similar to the one being valued. The comparables can then, when considered as a basket, give an indication of what the future value of a current business might be. For example, the market cap of a basket of five to 10 companies within a sector similar to a company under consideration could each be $500 million to $1 billion, and each could have growth rates of between 10 percent and 20 percent and certain commonalities in terms of EBITDA. The investor could conclude, based on the business plan and revenue model of the contemplated investment, that within two to three years the company under consideration should have the capability to develop a profile similar to this basket of companies. The investor could also determine what the likely valuation for the company under consideration would be in two to three years based on these comparables.

§ 4:5 The benefit of a contemplated strategic acquisition

In addition to comparing public market comparables, investors can examine recent strategic or private sales. The challenge in predicting the value of a strategic sale is in aggregating data that is helpful. The number of transactions in the area of strategic sales is in some cases too limited in a specific sector to provide a reliable prediction of a likely value for a company. If a venture investor is comfortable with the available data for comparable strategic sales in a sector, he will consider the multiple of price to revenue or price to EBITDA for these comparable companies and calculate a future value at the time of expected sale. The investor will then discount the projected value of the investor's ownership position at the expected time of the future sale to the present to determine the current value of the company.

Strategic sales are more common in certain industries and sectors and therefore more likely to be a compelling factor in determining a valuation if the probability of an acquisition is high. Larger companies may have net margins of say 10 percent, whereas a smaller company may have margins of say 20 to 30 percent. A company that is trading at a multiple of 10 times on the public markets and has margins of 10 percent can, for example, find a smaller company with margins of 20 to 30 percent that is growing at a rate of 15 to 20 percent particularly attractive. An acquisition creates a positive effect to the earnings of the larger company. The blended margins of the larger company will naturally improve with the acquisition of the smaller company.

Like small companies, firms with service-based business models are by nature likely to generate particularly high profit margins. They are, therefore, attractive acquisition candidates for public companies or large private companies looking either to expand their offerings or to improve their earnings. Take, for example, a computer hardware company that is looking to improve its offering through the acquisition or growth of a services business that provides professional services along with its hardware offering. Professional services businesses typically have margins of sometimes 20 to 30 percent, whereas hardware companies just in the business of selling hardware may have margins of 10 percent or less. This is why companies like Hewlett Packard and others have built out their services businesses. Companies dependent upon showing high margins of incremental growth often must pay a premium for companies with high growth rates. So the challenge for an early stage company is in positioning itself as an attractive acquisition candidate in its sector of business. The range of strategic acquisitions that may be available as comparables in a specific sector will, however, represent a range of valuations that may be a function of the varying strategic objectives of the acquirers. For this reason, it is unlikely that entrepreneurs and investors will agree on the same range of strategic sales as likely predictors in determining the future value of a company. Given the range of approaches to selecting comparables, it is therefore not surprising that the valuations expected by entrepreneurs and those offered by venture firms differ.

§ 4:6 When there are no comparables

There are times when the company being valued has no direct comparables and is a maverick. History tells us to focus on the fundamentals in these cases. The late 1990's and the period when the first round of Internet backed companies were funded perhaps provides a reasonable best road map. Companies that shot for the stars with unproven and unchallenged business models were quickly brought back to earth and required by their investors to focus on fundamentals like cash flow and profitability. In these instances it is perfectly plausible to class an investment, even if is a maverick, as broadly within a sector and to gauge its future value based on a multiple of revenues or EBITDA at some future point in time. The challenge in these instances is in getting an entrepreneur and an investor to agree on which comparables are fair.

§ 4:7 A wrinkle in valuations

The other wrinkle in determining valuation is in considering what truly will be required to get a company to become cash-flow positive and to position the company as an attractive candidate for a sale or IPO. Entrepreneurs and their boards may differ on their assumptions as to the pace and nature of growth that a company should pursue. Whereas one might contemplate two stages of financing, the likely valuation of a future financing will be subject to market factors, the financial performance of the company, and the profile of the management team at a future point in time. Often what is built into a current valuation will be the assumption of several financings prior to a possible sale or public offering.

An entrepreneur may lay out a plan that does not contemplate a future financing, whereas a VC may build a model that clearly assumes this as a possibility. The company has to ensure that its business model considers the worst case: fierce competition, price erosion, decrease in demand, dramatic changes in costs of distribution channels, and a longer-than-expected sales cycle.

For these reasons, it is incumbent on a venture investor to make assumptions that contemplate future financing even when an entrepreneur's plan may not include such financings. This may suggest that venture investors and entrepreneurs don't often see eye to eye on a company's business plan. To the contrary, the process of agreeing on a valuation often involves honest and candid discussions between an entrepreneur and an investor that result in more tempered and perhaps more realistic revenue models. On the other hand, the VCs that are notorious for being aggressive in their valuations but have remained in business have done so by operating with the expectation that their investments will take longer to harvest and more capital than it may appear.

This may not be something that an entrepreneur will want to agree to or accept, because by nature entrepreneurs and CEOs of fast-running companies need to believe in their plans. But it is perfectly reasonable and rational for any objective bystander to say that the course of the company and its business plan, by the nature of business, might need to change. And herein lies the essence of what hopefully will be a source of positive rather than negative tension between entrepreneur and investor.

Chapter 5

What Every Entrepreneur Needs to Know About Term Sheets

§ 5:1 Key areas of concern

While valuations are critical to setting in place a road map for future financings, a number of other areas of a term sheet require an entrepreneur's close attention as he or she looks to negotiate terms, gain leverage, or simply finalize the funding.

§ 5:2 Fees

Economics can be significantly affected by the language that addresses legal fees, placement fees, transaction fees, and finder's fees. This language typically appears in the last sections of the term sheet. It may not reveal the exact dollar amount of those fees, but may simply state that the company bear the cost of whatever fees may arise. It is critical therefore to clarify any language pertaining to intermediaries. Placement agents, for example, often require fees of up to 5 percent of the cash raised by a financing and in the region of the equivalent of 5 percent of the value of the round in warrants. Because placement agents are typically engaged by a company seeking financing, their fees should not come as a surprise. Finders fees can however become an issue; a VC may have learned of an investment through an intermediary and have an obligation to offer that intermediary a fee or an opportunity to earn equity in the contemplated investment.

§ 5:3 The crossroads to liquidity

The liquidation section of the term sheet spells out that in the case of the company's liquidation, preferred investors will require some multiple on their investment before common investors share in the proceeds from that liquidation. For example, if a company is raising $10 million in preferred stock, the investors might say that in the case of liquidation, the preferred will first be paid their original investment and any dividends out of proceeds and then will share on an as-converted basis the remaining proceeds with common investors. If an 8 percent cumulative dividend had been declared but not paid in each of three years on the preferred and the company is sold for $12.4 million, the preferred would receive all of the proceeds of the sale and the common would receive nothing. If the company were sold for $40 million and the preferred owned 40 percent of the company, the preferred would receive their initial $12.4 million plus 40 percent of the remaining proceeds, or $11.04 million, and the common would receive 60 percent of the remaining proceeds, or $16.56 million.

From the venture investor's perspective, this approach is eminently fair. In fact a 2.34 times return for the VC on original invested capital is not hot by VC standards. If we assume that the common paid 50 cents per share, their return is more like 2.2 times—not far behind that of the VC. But the extent to which this approach is fair from an entrepreneur's or common shareholder's perspective is purely a function of the entrepreneur's ownership position in the company, his or her cost basis for that ownership, and the likelihood of the company reaching its revenue target and break-even cash flow without needing a subsequent financing as well as likely exit values for the company.

§ 5:4 Liquidation versus conversion

Depending upon the terms that are negotiated, there is a point at which conversion to common by the preferred makes sense. If a cap has been negotiated so that the preferred is only able to receive a multiple on its original investment, of say three times, after which all proceeds go to the common, there is great incentive, and we consider again the example of the investor who purchases 40 percent of a company for $10 million, the preferred would likely have an incentive to convert to common when proceeds exceed $75 million. Consider a scenario wherein the net proceeds from the likely sale of a company are $80 million and there is a cap of three times including declared but unpaid dividends for the preferred. The preferred would be due no more than $30 million, three times their $10 million investment; and the common would have rights to the remaining $50 million in proceeds. Let's assume instead that the preferred were to convert to common and, per a requirement of conversion under the terms negotiated, must waive rights to its declared but unpaid dividend in order to convert to common. Under this scenario conversion would generate $32 million in proceeds, the common equivalent proceeds for an ownership position of 40% of $80 million.

The comparison of liquidation preference versus conversion is a good litmus test for entrepreneurs looking to get a clear indication of the value an investor is looking for as a minimum and at what point a company's performance will generate returns for everybody that more than exceed minimum expectations.

§ 5:5 Balancing expectations and requirements

The next issue for the entrepreneur is balancing his desire to optimize the terms of a financing with the fact that he has been offered a term sheet that represents his potential financing partner's requirements. Because the context of every financing is subject to so many variables—an investor's assessment of and appetite for risk, the stage of the company within the sector in which it is focused, and the profile of the management team to name a few—predicting the appropriate balance between the desires of both parties in any one case is simply not possible. If there is anything that feels too complicated or inappropriate when considering the context and stage or profile of an investment, a warning bell should probably go off. Milestones may be appropriate, for example, for companies that are predicting aggressive growth but have little in their history to indicate likelihood of achieving that growth. With an experienced management team that is looking for a small amount of funding and that has countless examples of customers in-hand who are predictive of the acceptance of a business model by new customers, milestones may be inappropriate.

Therefore, the maxim "know and understand your customer" certainly applies when analyzing the motivations and desires of the investor who has presented a term sheet. If entrepreneur and investor agree on the value of the business being built, if the funding history and the momentum of the firm have been clean and without speed bumps, and the risk associated with the investment in the investor's mind is relatively low, there shouldn't be too many complicated terms. Nevertheless, there may be terms that are unique to and typical of the way the investor works. No matter what the flavor of term sheet, it is important to work with an experienced lawyer who knows these types of deals. If the lawyer feels that there are unusual terms, the entrepreneur should first explore with the VC or investor why the terms have been presented. The entrepreneur should treat a first discussion about the term sheet as an opportunity to learn more about his partner. If that discussion becomes a negotiation and terms seem unreasonable, it would be appropriate to include experienced counsel in a discussion or negotiation.

§ 5:6 Exercising control

The control that investors may look for should typically empower them to ensure that a company's business plan is followed and that a company is performing to expectation and to plan. Entrepreneurs should closely examine the Protective Provisions, Board Composition and Meetings, Special Board Approval Items sections as well as any milestones. Where these provisions are not aligned with the goals and projected needs as outlined in the company's business plan, they should be questioned (or, if acceptable to the entrepreneur, the business plan altered). These sections and tools may have the intended effect of giving investors the power to link an entrepreneur and his management team's future with the company and with the company's performance. The way in which powers are either articulated or actually exercised will significantly impact the flexibility and independence of the management team when reaching their goals and targets.

§ 5:7 The option of stock options

Stock options, the way stock options will be issued, and the size of the overall stock option pool should also be an area of concern for entrepreneurs. Whether or not a Post Financing Capitalization Table is built into a term sheet, an entrepreneur should keep an intimate knowledge of his cap table. If the pool of stock options that has been created before a contemplated round is not sufficient to enable the company to provide key employees with a competitive options package, the way in which an options pool is increased as part of a financing is critical to the economic value of the round that evolves. It would be typical that options and warrants outstanding, whether issued or unissued, are included in the pre-money valuation. It would also be understandable that investors would expect that a sufficient number of options will be issued either before or after the financing to satisfy the need to incentivize staff once the round is closed. Clearly, issuance of options is dilutive. Term sheet pricing that assumes that options will be issued after a round is closed may therefore typically be cheaper than term sheet pricing that assumes an adequate number of options exist so that no new options will have to be created either before or after the contemplated round is closed.

Entrepreneurs must therefore clearly understand how an options plan will affect valuations and the pricing of financings. This will allow them to avoid situations in which an investor has agreed to a certain pre-money valuation, joins a board after a financing goes through, and then becomes less flexible as a firm's options plan begins to call for issuance of additional numbers of shares that had never been contemplated at the time of the prior financing. With this in mind, it should not be surprising that investors may question vesting schedules, ask that they be revisited at the time of a financing, or require that new contracts for certain employees be put in place before a closing is executed. Vesting schedules are typically four years, but terms can be accelerated to three or extended to five.

§ 5:8 What not to do in a negotiation

There are many terms to watch for; depending upon market conditions, most are negotiable. But one thing an entrepreneur should never do is negotiate terms without understanding the term sheet in its entirety. Consult a lawyer before deciding to negotiate it yourself. Venture firms spend a great deal of time and resources in drafting a term sheet. Attempting to negotiate without fully understanding how the parts of a term sheet interact will either reveal an entrepreneur's weakness in a negotiation or test the patience of investors.

Even if the entrepreneur has been trained in the law, he still should involve someone with legal expertise and an understanding of the broader marketplace in any negotiation of a term sheet once it is accepted. As company's counsel will ultimately need to review or draft the documents that are produced once the term sheet is agreed upon, it is just smarter to get the same advice during the term sheet stage. The entrepreneur will also look more professional during any negotiation with investors, and rather than test an investor's patience, have a higher likelihood of working a negotiation to the company's advantage.

Negotiation is certainly an opportunity to improve terms, but it's also an opportunity to improve the governance and discipline of the company. Entrepreneurs should respect that the best venture firms have consistently used similar terms and set similar expectations in their term sheets, presumably to the success of their companies as much as for their own benefit. Trying to dramatically change the term sheet of a venture firm is like saying you don't like the way they work. There will be different partners at venture firms who all have different ways of operating and communicating. But if it's a good firm, the terms should not be grossly different when compared to other deals of similar profiles done by the firm. There are always exceptions, but most of the time terms from the same firm will have a level of consistency from term sheet to term sheet.

§ 5:9 Unusual requests

It is possible, however, to see an unusual request made by an investor. These are often called outliers. They can simply indicate a characteristic unique to the firm's approach, not one that is necessarily unique to the firm's negotiation with the entrepreneur. Outliers are typically instituted because of fiduciary guidelines unique to one firm or because the market environment is moving the firm to require particularly investor-friendly terms.

The requirement to be able to perform a forensic audit is one example. The ability to require a forensic audit provides an investor with the opportunity to conduct a complete audit of a company's activities. It may be performed by an accounting team, members of the venture firm, or by a corporate investor's own staff. The purpose would be to ensure that significant contracts and corresponding performance obligations or expectations are legitimate, and to audit the company's performance against milestones, which may have been set in contracts, as well as to make sure the firm isn't "cooking its books." In essence, it's post-investment due diligence; an annual full audit of the balance sheet and off balance sheet risks, and an attempt to validate a company's cash burn rate and to review internal controls. Such a request is typically representative of a set of policies that have been put in place by an investment firm or several firms.

Another example of an outlier could be the type of fees paid to an investor as part of a transaction or additional fees related to his or her activities serving on the board or in other capacities for the company. Certain deal fees could be charged the company and justified as transaction expenses. For larger funds it is typical that companies will pay expenses related to a board member's travel and accommodation for board meetings. But there is a class of small funds whose size is so small that the economics of such funds will assume that board participation and transaction fees will supplement fund fee income.

§ 5:10 Creating partnerships

The chemistry and type of partnership that evolves and reveals itself during the initial due diligence and term sheet process will set the tone for the type of relationship that will transpire thereafter. The best relationships between a firm and a portfolio company begin with a complete review and understanding of a business plan and how the firm expects to execute. Term sheets should not be about long and protracted negotiation processes; they are about having spent enough time at a company to really understand the opportunity it presents, to learn the basics of the politics and existing shareholders issues and objectives, and to present a term sheet that works with those criteria.

For entrepreneurs, a large and important part of deciding whether and how much to negotiate is understanding the style of the partner or group of partners with whom they are working. Although an entrepreneur may always speak with only one representative of a VC firm, there are typically several partners who he has never met who are involved in the review of a company and wield significant influence. So, the entrepreneur needs to understand the venture firm's process and the way in which its terms are drafted and presented.

In most cases, it is to be expected that there will be certain issues that will always be unique to each prospective portfolio company that require negotiation. But by the time a term sheet is presented to a company, the majority of the economics have already been discussed by a venture firm and the partners responsible for a deal. Even with some give and take, the nature of the term sheet that is initially presented is not going to be wildly different from the negotiated final document.

But some firms don't work that way at all. They will float a term sheet before much of the due diligence work on the deal is done by the firm and submit a term sheet with the intention of getting the entrepreneur to commit to a relationship before seriously researching the opportunity. The process that follows is a period of negotiation and simultaneous due diligence. The risk involved from the company's perspective and the venture firm's perspective is that the nature of the relationship will not be really clear until after the negotiation has transpired and that disagreements which may follow result in irreconcilable differences.

§ 5:11 Simultaneous deals

In some cases an entrepreneur will negotiate several term

sheets simultaneously. In these situations, investors may vary in their willingness to negotiate.

When investors agree with entrepreneurs about the prospects for their company, the investors may come close to meeting the expectations of the prospective portfolio company regarding expected valuation. This assumes that the investors have taken the time to meet and understand the position of existing stakeholders. If what follows is a protracted set of negotiations in which the entrepreneur works with several other firms simultaneously to develop several other term sheets, the investor to submit the first term sheet may not on principle be willing to change its original position until the company commits to select them. The whole term sheet process is in a way a test of the type of relationship that is likely to be consummated in a financing. So why would an investor float a term sheet if there is a risk that it may be shopped? The typical expectation is that the entrepreneur who said he would like to work them, because of the added value they may bring or their firm may bring, has done so in good faith. The assumption is that if the entrepreneur identifies another firm that has complementary strengths, that the entrepreneur will consider working with both of them if the capital required would warrant participation by two firms. If a second firm provides a higher valuation, they can only trust that the entrepreneur will be open with them and, if new information warrants a higher valuation or the valuation should be revisited, that they will be given the opportunity to do so.

§ 5:12 East coast versus west coast rules

While the term sheets' general formats and styles may not vary significantly from firm to firm, there are many variables in terms of legal language that can be changed and substituted; and the effective result can vary significantly.

Traditionally, people have considered West Coast terms to be written more loosely and fluidly than East Coast terms. East Coast terms are known to be a little tighter and more conservative. This is not to say that the lawyers in the West Coast are not equally thorough and conscientious. This is just a generalization in terms of a way of differentiating two styles.

There are a few areas in which East Coast and West Coast rules vary significantly. One area is dividends. West Coast firms may encourage clients to consider cumulative dividends whereas East Coast firms may be comfortable with non-cumulative dividends. Another area of differentiation between the Coasts is the way in which anti-dilution clauses are calculated. The two different formulas that can be used are broad-based or narrow-based. An anti-dilution clause that is broad-based will take stock options into account. The California standard is broad-based and could affect a 6 to 7 percent higher value for existing shareholders in the event of dilution when compared to the East Coast standard.

Another approach attributable to West Coast firms are pay-to-play rules. New investors can be harsh and require that in future rounds, current investors will need to maintain their pro-rata share of investment—continue to invest so that their shareholding percentage remains the same. Such rules would dictate that if they don't, their share holding position may be diluted significantly. The pay-to-play term is a significant requirement of investors. But it is not uncommon at an early stage in a deal, because people are saying: "Look, this deal has a significant amount of risk, it might take longer to execute than we envision, and we don't want to get in as a lead investor unless everyone else recognizes this risk."

APPENDIX A

Exhibit

[insert name of company]

Summary of Terms for Proposed Private

Placement of Convertible Preferred Stock

Issuer:	_______ ("Company").
Investors:	____, _______ and ____ ("Investors").
Current Outstanding Securities	____ shares of Common Stock: ("Common") and options to purchase __________________ shares of Common.
Amount of Investment:	$_______.
Type of Security:	Series A Convertible Preferred Stock ("Preferred").
Number of Shares:	_______.
Price per Share:	$_______ ("Original Purchase Price").

Rights, Preferences, Privileges and Restrictions of Preferred:	(1) Dividend Provisions: A cumulative dividend on the Preferred will accrue at the rate of $________ per share per annum ("Accruing Dividends"). Accruing Dividends will be payable only (a) if, as and when determined by the Board of Directors ("Board") or (b) upon the liquidation or winding up of the Company. [For dividends equivalent to Common dividends, substitute the following sentence for the two preceding sentences: The same dividend per share will be paid on the Preferred as is paid on the Common (with the Preferred being treated as equivalent to the number of shares of Common into which it is convertible).] No dividend will be paid on the Common, and no shares of Common will be repurchased by the Company except for unvested shares repurchased from former employees at their original purchase price.

(2) Liquidation Preference: In the event of the liquidation or winding up of the Company, the holders of Preferred will be entitled to receive in preference to the holders of Common an amount equal to the greater of (a) the Original Purchase Price plus any dividends accrued on the Preferred but not paid or (b) the amount they would have received had they converted the Preferred to Common immediately prior to such liquidation or winding up. [For participating Preferred, substitute the following two sentences for the preceding sentence: In the event of the liquidation or winding up of the Company, the holders of Preferred will be entitled to receive in preference to the holders of Common an amount ("Liquidation Amount") equal to the Original Purchase Price plus any dividends accrued on the Preferred but not paid. After the Liquidation Amount has been paid, the holders of Preferred and Common will be entitled to receive the remaining assets, with the Preferred being treated as equivalent to the number of shares of Common into which it is convertible.]

A consolidation or merger of the Company or sale of all or substantially all of its assets will be deemed to be a liquidation or winding up for purposes of the liquidation preference.

(3) Redemption: On ___, the Company will redeem the Preferred by paying in cash the Original Purchase Price plus any dividends (excluding Accruing Dividends) accrued on the Preferred but not paid. [For redemptions payable in installments, substitute the following sentence for the preceding sentence: On each of ___, ___, and ___ the Company will redeem one-third of the Preferred originally issued by paying in cash the Original Purchase Price plus any dividends (excluding Accruing Dividends) accrued on the Preferred but not paid.] If the Company fails to redeem the Preferred when due, the conversion price of the Preferred thereafter will decrease at the rate of 10% per quarter and the holders of the Preferred will be entitled to elect a majority of the directors.

(4) Conversion: A holder of Preferred will have the right to convert the Preferred, at the option of the holder, at any time, into shares of Common. The total number of shares of Common into which the Preferred may be converted initially will be determined by dividing the Original Purchase Price by the conversion price. The initial conversion price will be the Original Purchase Price. The conversion price will be subject to adjustment as provided in paragraph (3) above and paragraph (6) below.

(5) Automatic Conversion: The Preferred will be automatically converted into Common, at the then applicable conversion price, in the event of an underwritten public offering of shares of the Common at a public offering price per share that is not less than $______ in an offering of not less than $______.

(6) Antidilution Provisions: If the Company issues additional shares (other than the Reserved Shares described under "Reserved Shares" below) at a purchase price less than the applicable conversion price, the conversion price of the Preferred will be reduced to such lower price in order to prevent dilution. [For weighted average antidilution, replace the foregoing with: If the Company issues additional shares (other than the Reserved Shares described under "Reserved Shares" below) at a purchase price less than the applicable conversion price, the conversion price of the Preferred will be reduced on a weighted average formula basis to diminish the effect of such dilutive issuance on the Preferred.]

(7) Voting Rights: Except with respect to election of directors and certain protective provisions, the holders of Preferred will have the right to that number of votes equal to the number of shares of Common issuable upon conversion of the Preferred. Election of directors and the protective provisions will be as described under "Board Representation and Meetings" and "Protective Provisions," respectively, below.

(8) Protective Provisions: Consent of the holders of at least two-thirds of the Preferred will be required for (i) any sale by the Company of substantially all of its assets, (ii) any merger of the Company with another entity, (iii) any liquidation or winding up of the Company, (iv) any amendment of the Company's charter or by-laws [any amendment of the Company's charter or by-laws that is adverse to the Preferred], or (v) certain other actions materially affecting the Preferred.

Information Rights:	So long as any of the Preferred is outstanding, the Company will deliver to each Investor annual, quarterly and monthly financial statements, annual budgets and other information reasonably requested by an Investor.
Registration Rights:	(1) Demand Rights: If, at any time after the earlier of the Company's initial public offering and the date three years from the purchase of the Preferred (but not within 6 months of the effective date of a registration), Investors holding at least 40% of the Common issued or issuable upon conversion of the Preferred request that the Company file a Registration Statement covering at least 20% of the Common issued or issuable upon conversion of the Preferred (or any lesser percentage if the anticipated aggregate offering price would exceed \$5,000,000), the Company will use its best efforts to cause such shares to be registered. The Company will not be obligated to effect more than two registrations (other than on Form S-3) under these demand right provisions.

(2) Registrations on Form S-3: Holders of Common issued or issuable upon conversion of the Preferred will have the right to require the Company to file an unlimited number of Registration Statements on Form S-3 (or any equivalent successor form), provided the anticipated aggregate offering price in each registration on Form S-3 will exceed $1,000,000.

(3) Piggy-Back Registration: The Investors will be entitled to "piggy-back" registration rights on registrations of the Company, subject to the right of the Company and its underwriters to reduce in view of market conditions the number of shares of the Investors proposed to be registered to not less than one-third of the total number of shares in the offering.

(4) Registration Expenses: The registration expenses (exclusive of underwriting discounts and commissions) of all of the registrations under paragraphs (1), (2) and (3) above will be borne by the Company.

(5) Transfer of Registration Rights: The registration rights may be transferred to a transferee who acquires at least 20% of an Investor's shares. Transfer of registration rights to a partner or shareholder of any Investor will be without restriction as to minimum shareholding.

(6) Other Registration Provisions: Other provisions will be contained in the Purchase Agreement with respect to registration rights as are reasonable, including cross-indemnification, the Company's ability to delay the filing of a demand registration for a period of not more than 90 days in certain circumstances, the agreement by the Investors (if requested by the underwriters in a public offering) not to sell any unregistered Common they hold for a period of 120 days following the effective date of the Registration Statement of such offering, the period of time in which the Registration Statement will be kept effective, underwriting arrangements and the like.

	(7) No Registration of Preferred: The registration rights set forth herein apply only to the Common and the Company will never be obligated to register any of the Preferred.
Use of Proceeds:	The proceeds from the sale of the Preferred will be used for working capital.

Board Representation and Meetings:	The charter will provide that the authorized number of directors is ________________. The Preferred (voting as a class) will elect ________________ directors, the Common (voting as a class) will elect ________________ directors, and the remaining director will be such person, if any, who has received a plurality of the votes of both the Preferred and the Common (voting as separate classes) [and the remaining directors will be elected by the Preferred and the Common voting together as a single class]. The Board will meet at least quarterly. The bylaws will provide, in addition to any provisions required by law, that any two directors or holders of at least 25% of the Preferred may call a meeting of the Board. Investors holding at least ____ shares of Preferred will be entitled to have an observer attend Board meetings. Effective upon the purchase of the Preferred, the members of the Board will be ______, ______ and ______.
Key Person Insurance:	$______ on each of ____, ____ and ____, with the proceeds payable to the Company.

Right of First Offer for Purchase of New Securities:	So long as any of the Preferred is outstanding, if if the Company proposes to offer any shares for the purpose of financing its business (other than Reserved Shares, shares issued in the acquisition of another company, or shares offered to the public pursuant to an underwritten public offering), the Company will first offer all such shares to the Investors. [For true preemptive right, replace the foregoing with: So long as any of the Preferred is outstanding, if the Company proposes to offer any shares for the purpose of financing its business (other than Reserved Shares, shares issued in the acquisition of another company, or shares offered to the public pursuant to an underwritten public offering), the Company will first offer a portion of such shares to the Investors so as to enable them to maintain their percentage interest in the Company.]

Stock Restriction Agreements: ___, ___ and ___ will each execute a Stock Restriction Agreement with the Investors and the Company pursuant to which the Investors will have a right of first refusal with respect to any shares proposed to be sold by such persons. The Stock Restriction Agreement will also contain a right of co-sale providing that before any such person may sell any of his shares, he will first give the Investors an opportunity to participate in such sale on a basis proportionate to the amount of securities held by the seller and those held by the Investors. In addition, the Stock Restriction Agreement will restrict such person from selling more than ______% of his shares for ___ years from the purchase of the Preferred. The Stock Restriction Agreement will also give the Company the right to repurchase such person's unvested shares at a price equal to his original purchase price, in the event his employment with the Company terminates. Shares will vest at the rate of ______% per annum. The Stock Restriction Agreement will terminate after ten years or, if earlier, an underwritten public offering of the Common in an amount of at least $______.

Reserved Shares:	The Company currently has ___ shares of Common reserved for issuance to directors, officers, employees and consultants upon the exercise of outstanding options. The Company may reserve up to ___ additional shares of Common for issuance to such persons. (Such ___ shares already reserved, and the additional shares, are referred to as the “Reserved Shares”.)

	The Reserved Shares will be issued from time to time to directors, officers, employees and consultants of the Company (other than ____) under such arrangements, contracts or plans as are recommended by management and approved by the Board, provided that without the unanimous consent of the directors elected solely by the Preferred, the vesting of any such shares (or options therefor) issued to any such person shall not be at a rate in excess of 20% per annum from the date of issuance. Unless subsequently agreed to the contrary by the Investors, any issuance of shares in excess of the Reserved Shares will be a dilutive event requiring adjustment of the conversion price as provided above and will be subject to the Investors' first offer right as described above. Holders of Reserved Shares who are officers or employees of the Company will be required to execute Stock Restriction Agreements generally as described above.
Noncompetition Agreement:	____, ____ and ____ will each enter into a noncompetition agreement with the Company in a form reasonably acceptable to the Investors.

Nondisclosure and Developments Agreement:	Each officer and key employee of the Company will enter into a nondisclosure and developments agreement in a form reasonably acceptable to the Investors.

The Purchase Agreement:	The purchase of the Preferred will be made pursuant to a Series A Convertible Preferred Stock Purchase Agreement drafted by counsel to the Investors. Such agreement shall contain, among other things, appropriate representations and warranties of the Company, covenants of the Company reflecting the provisions set forth herein and other typical covenants, and appropriate conditions of closing, including, among other things, qualification of the shares under applicable Blue Sky laws, the filing of a certificate of amendment to the Company's charter to authorize the Preferred, and an opinion of counsel. Until the Purchase Agreement is signed by both the Company and the Investors, there will not exist any binding obligation on the part of either party to consummate the transaction. This Summary of Terms does not constitute a contractual commitment of the Company or the Investors or an obligation of either party to negotiate with the other.

Expenses:	The Company and the Investors will each bear their own legal and other expenses with respect to the transaction (except that, assuming a successful completion of the transaction, the Company will pay the legal fees and expenses of ________, counsel to the Investors).
Finders:	The Company and the Investors will each indemnify the other for any finder's fees for which either is responsible.